T0171028

in Grandma's *Shoes*

Multigenerational Memoirs

Bonnie DiMichele

BALBOA.
PRESS

A DIVISION OF HAY HOUSE

Balboa Press books may be ordered through booksellers or by contacting:

Balboa Press
A Division of Hay House
1663 Liberty Drive
Bloomington, IN 47403
www.balboapress.com
1 (877) 407-4847

Printed in the United States of America.

ISBN: 978-1-4525-8837-7 (sc)
ISBN: 978-1-4525-8865-0 (e)

Library of Congress Control Number: 2013922383

Balboa Press rev. date: 1/15/2014

The little village of Stony Creek, Connecticut is a section of the town of Branford and is in the county of New Haven. It sits between Guilford and East Haven and is home to the Thimble Islands.

To my husband John who

takes all my adventures

with me, and my children,

Nikki, John, & Matt

who light up my life.

To those future generations

who may seek answers

to my past,

Bella, Dom, and

those we've yet

to meet.

Contents

Preface

It was upon asking my husband, the other day, to describe his childhood in one or two words, that I realized that life is full of inquiry if we just search for it. His response was, "educational," and that filled me with wonder. I would never express my childhood in that manner. How very wonderful that he thought that his childhood was that way, and I asked him to expand upon that thought. It is through these sorts of conversations that we learn much about others but perhaps even more about ourselves. My descriptive word was, "bittersweet." I am aware that the bitter part of that is not a good place to hold on to. I choose to remember the sweet part of growing up. In doing so, I may be able to leave the, not so fond, memories behind.

A few holiday cards ago, I asked what friends and families fondest childhood thought was. My mother answered me with, "my favorite thoughts happened after I met your father." I asked her to seriously contemplate her answer. Surely there was one favorite time or one favorite memory that she did as a child that filled her with happy thoughts. She again said that her childhood was impoverished and not pleasant and that her happiest times were with my father. "Life had become better with him." I respected her feelings and found that I understood her patience with him in a way that I had not appreciated before.

In finding my grandmother's travel diary a few years ago, tucked in with the old family photos, I found that I had a hundred questions or more about who she truly was. My image of her was as an old lady. A lovely old lady, but an old lady, nonetheless. I realized that I was about her age when she took this trip to the place that she had grown-up in, and that was of great interest to me. She had left behind a clue to who she really was and how she really viewed the world. I believe that she took such pains in preparing it so that she could relive or revisit her trip to Connecticut any time she wished. There, in those two little old greeting card boxes, lay the person that my grandmother remembered being. I think that her trip brought her visual and sensory memories that she could only renew by stepping foot on the land where she had experienced childhood imagination. I do think that she also hoped that her family would desire to read and see her account one day. That day never came; but it was not wasted on me. I fully love that she took the time to document those things important to her. I only wish that she could have taken the photos in color. She would have loved to have those memories in color.

I often wish that she had shared her experiences with me. By the time I came along, she seemed tired and a bit weary of the silliness of young minds. I worry that our society is losing the art of conversation with our cell phones, tweets, and texts. Our life experiences are so much more than a simple word or trendy phrase. When we open up to people around us, we find that we have many common experiences, loves, trials, and wishes. I am exercising my right to unplug and artfully use one-on-one communication so I can have meaningful relationships with those people who are most important to me. Technology is a wonderful tool but I don't want to be emotionally left out in the dark, (should the electrical plug ever get pulled).

The Building Years

I've realized today, that it has been 33 years 8 months and 5 days since my grandmother passed away. I was nearly 23 at the time and remember how very frail she was when I would visit her in the convalescent home after her stroke. Frail was never a word I would have used to describe my grandmother. She was very tall, as I was very small, she seemed so very large (often weighing well over 200 pounds), and appeared to be perpetually working hard, taking little time for the things I found fun in life. She had pale white skin that was pillowy and very soft to the touch. I would often find her cooking in her tiny galley style kitchen or canning fruits and vegetables to stock away in her equally long pantry. She'd designed the house on 30th Ave. in Santa Cruz, California herself, and the pantry, as well as it's contents, was her pride and joy.

My grandmother, Ruth Chidsey Bates Lewis, had come through the long, hungry years of the depression in Banning, California while raising a family, so canning had become a necessity of life. The family had moved from Riverside, California because there were jobs in Banning, surrounding the water line that was being brought to Los Angeles County and it's surrounding basin. She'd worked at a cannery sorting fruit and was allowed to bring the bad fruit home after her shift. She'd stay up late into the night cutting, slicing, and canning so her five children would have something to eat. She and my grandfather had lost their rental properties during the depression because the tenants couldn't pay the rent. Luckily for my grandparents, they had built a stone home by gathering stones from the wash in Banning. They had, upon borrowing $500.00 (worth about $6,4000.00 today) from Grandma's grandmother, purchased a new truck and had driven back and forth from the San Gorgonio Mountain wash, to fill the rear of the pickup with sand for mortar and river rock for the walls of the home they were building together. I am told that the truck wasn't looking very new upon completion of the house. They designed and built that home together, placing each and every stone in it's proper place, and it was fully paid for by the time the depression hit. They lost the rental properties that the bank held but were fortunate enough to maintain their family home.

In a photo that my grandmother took she wrote <u>1925 our first stone house</u>. My grandfather was a carpenter and he had built this house for a wealthy gentleman in the town. I believe that, as my grandfather helped to build this house, it prompted him to realize that they could build their own stone house, and they did just that. It was next door and not nearly as beautiful as the craftsman style home Grandpa had built first. Both of these houses are still standing today, as are the wooden rental houses my grandfather had built. There is a short chain-link fence that surrounds both of the stone houses and they don't hold the quaintness that I found in this photo. I took my parents past these houses several years ago with the hope that they were still standing. Standing they were, but not nearly as lovely. I'd put my photo of the newer version, of the craftsman style house here, but I want to remember it as it was meant to be; not as the hideous remodeled version some other family thought it should be. (Craftsman houses should never be painted bright blue.) That's the wonderful thing about selective memories; we can mold them into what we want them to be. We can hold on to the unpleasant happenings as horrible things that play over and over in our minds or we can seek to find the pleasantness of every event that is placed in our lives. It's a personal choice really; look for joy or dwell on negatives. For me it's an easy choice; always search for the positive.

The craftsman house was not my grandparent's but this little stone house on the left, was the very house my father first grew up in. They had started out in the house on the right, but it wasn't a house at the time; it was a garage. My grandfather put a little stone water feature under the front window for my grandmother. They got very tired of trying to keep fish in this pond, as the birds would come by and feast on the fish. It was hard enough to put food on the table for the family, let alone creating food for the birds that would wonder by. Upon completion of the stone house next door, they moved from the garage and had an indoor bathroom and much more room for the five children. They had a very small basement area for their canned goods and a desert cooler. The desert cooler was placed outside as there wasn't refrigeration at the time. The coolness of the water, dripping from the garden hose, would moistened the burlap sacks, that were placed over the racks. That water would not only eventually reach the flowers to water them but would also keep the chicken eggs cool. Life was much more comfortable in this house. Banning looks like a hot, dry area, as you travel past it on the highway, but it is actually a little cooler than the valley floor as it is slightly elevated. I haven't been too taken with it, the few times that I have visited and my grandma wasn't terribly taken with it as well. It did prove to be a nice place to raise their family and they didn't move back down into Pomona until my father had graduated from Banning High School in 1943.

In 1935 my grandparent's also lost their only daughter, Vivian, who was their joy in life. She was 19, and also working at the cannery along side my grandmother to help the family survive. She suffered from appendicitis and they watched her fade away from them for three long excruciating days. There was nothing they could do but helplessly watch and realize the end was near. Whatever the depression had not taken from them was taken the day she passed away. That was years and a different town before I came along but I always remember my grandparents with silvery white hair, and I remember them as being, not terribly happy in life. I suppose their struggles and their grief caused their prematurely silvery hair color.

It is important to note that behind this little house were two other houses where my great grandmother, great grandfather, and great-great grandmother lived. My grandmother and the fore mentioned people had lost my grandmother's brother to exactly the same illness when he was 10, back in Stony Creek, Connecticut. These ladies all knew exactly what was happening around them and the heartbreak that they were all experiencing... well, it's my guess that they could barely speak of it. I can not imagine their pain.

Visitation

I remember spending time on 30th Ave. in Santa Cruz, California, not alone with Grandma and Grandpa, but along with my family. I was never left alone with my grandparents. Neither I, nor my two sisters can recall ever spending one-on-one time alone with either of them. Grandma was a solitary, yet pleasant woman, but Grandpa had a mean streak that was long and unforgiving. I've heard stories about my grandfather's quick temper but I seldom experienced it myself. I can tell you that my father always seemed to be on high alert as to what we were doing while visiting at our grandparent's house. He was that way too, when they would come to visit us at our house. Dad always seemed on edge when they were present. I suppose we were not left with our grandparents due to things that had transpired during my father's childhood. My uncles used to talk about how their dad would punish them with anything that was readily available. They often mentioned the use of hammers and pieces of wood. I can not imagine the brutality of these actions, nor did I see it as a child. I preferred to be outside when visiting them, and I distinctly remember that it seemed a safer place outside. There was a garden virtually surrounding the gigantic corner lot with plenty of room for fruit trees, vegetables, flowers, and rhubarb. Oh how they loved their strawberry rhubarb pie and Grandma made a great crust. I liked the crust ten times better than the pie filling. I was never quite sure if the filling was going to be sweet or sour and many times my mouth would crinkle into a pucker because it was so very sour.

There was an old, dusty, red, cobwebby, barn on the 30th Ave. property that had once housed chickens. It held the remnants of chicken feathers, wire, and lots of left over chicken poop near the rear of the lot. Grandpa had all sorts of interesting looking tools that were certainly well on their way to rusting beyond reasonable use. For a short time, in the barn, was where Alice the calf resided. Alice was a reddish Guernsey with a white face and head. I was so excited to see that Grandpa had a baby cow and being small, at the age of six, everyone would put me up on top of her and help me ride around the backyard. I loved that calf; what wasn't there to love about cows in general? I spent most of my days outside serenading the cows who grazed across the street from our house on High Street.

It was lonely up on High Street. We were out in the country on the west side of Santa Cruz. There weren't many neighbors, and my sisters were five and nine years older than myself. I spent most of my time outside, climbing trees, playing with cars and trucks in the sand pit, climbing up and down the drainage holes, catching my favorite tree frog, hanging upside down from the clothes line poles, hiding behind the block retaining wall, catching lizards, singing, and making up stories that only myself and the cows seemed to appreciate. So, what's not to like about cows? They look at you as if they sort of care that you too, are interested in them.

These are pictures of the first garden my grandparents had in Santa Cruz and they became better gardeners every passing year. Some of my first recollections of Grandma in her shoes, were when she was out working in the garden on that property. It looks as though they could have opened their own produce stand, and perhaps that was a thought of theirs as they had opened a stand while living in Los Angeles, on Figueroa St. I don't know why they gave that up but maybe the demands of a family of seven, plus three aging relatives claimed too much of their time.

When we would go to visit Grandma we would enter through the back door, which was attached to the screened-in back porch and the carport. Grandpa had put in poles and covered the carport with corrugated fiberglass. The sheets of fiberglass just lay simply across the poles and it never looked like that project had been completely finished. (It was a bit of an eye sore, really.) I always thought it funny that they had a front door because it was almost never used. Most of the time you would find the card table set up in the tiny entry with a working jigsaw puzzle on it. Jigsaw puzzles were the one thing that Grandma and Grandpa seemed to enjoy doing together, yet it was obvious that there were times when they wouldn't work on the puzzle for days, if not weeks, at a time. I didn't give it much thought when I was young, but I think they were arguing during those times. I just wanted to see a new puzzle so I could help them as it got towards the end. The pieces are so much easier to find near the end and I always felt so proud in helping them complete a puzzle.

Grandma had an organ in that front room and the walls were filled with Grandma's paintings. Unfortunately they are not the kind of prized paintings one might perceive being hung about Grandma's house. They were paint-by-number paintings. I've never seen a paint-by-number painting that looked like anything but a paint-by-number painting. She was so very proud of them and I would always tell her how beautiful they were. I thought they were not very realistic looking, but she would hide them from us until she could reveal the finished product. That finished product was always framed and freshly placed on the wall where it would be proudly displayed with all the other paint-by-number paintings. Grandpa proudly made all of the frames for her to house her paintings in. I wish she could have taken art classes. I think she would have loved that. She did take organ lessons at quite an advanced age and actually played for her church as she progressed. I never heard her play much, so I know little about her level of expertise. What was important to note about Grandma was her persistence in everything she did in life.

The above photo is of Grandma and Grandpa (known as Mom and Pop to some) at their 50th Wedding Anniversary party, held at their home. They are standing in front of some of her finest paint-by-number's.

Around the corner from the living room was the family room where the TV was. This, and the kitchen were the places we spent most of our time while visiting 30th Ave. Grandma had only put 1 bedroom in the house. I guess she didn't want us sleeping over. The pantry was almost as long as the kitchen and had a door on each end. The bathroom was equally as long as the pantry and had a door on each of it's ends, as well. I was always panic stricken that, one of the doors wouldn't be locked and someone would walk in on me while I was using the toilet. I found using the bathroom at Grandma's to be something I tried desperately to avoid. Across the hall from the long bathroom was the tiniest 1/2 bath I've ever seen. You could barely get inside and squeeze up against the tiny sink so you could close the door and squeeze yourself onto the seat so your knees wouldn't hit the back of the door. I was quite small at the time and found it almost as uncomfortable as the long bathroom, but with an entirely different feel of uneasiness. I don't think Grandma used the 1/2 bath; it just wouldn't have been worth the trouble. I suppose that every inch of that house plan needed to have a practical use in Grandma's mind, and thusly she stuck in a bathroom where a nice closet would have been an excellent touch. I remember also that Grandma had aluminum jalousie louvered windows installed in every room in that house. She had done that so she could open up the windows and have air flow through the house, a little venter y effect if you like. It was perfect for Santa Cruz as the fog would roll in and out about every day during the summer. The windows were not easy to see out of though because they had many lines in them from the louvers. I believe that these windows stopped being produced because they weren't secure enough from the outside. Grandma loved those windows and all the cool air they provided her. My husband and I drove by this house about three years ago to see what changes had been made to it. We couldn't see a thing! The entire property is now surrounded by fencing that is eight to ten feet tall. It made me wonder what was behind all that fencing.

Most of my time spent there, was outside under a weeping willow tree that was so lush and deep green, that it was a great place to lose myself in fantasy and imagination. I rarely visited the tree in winter when the branches were bare and it was too cold to play outside for long periods of time. I do remember standing beneath it wishing for spring to arrive so my private hiding spot would return. Later in my life I found an entrance to a friends mother's house that gave me the same feeling as that old weeping willow did. The drive to her house was lined with, what I call, tunnel trees.

Tunnel Trees

Summer, Winter,
Spring, & Fall,
There is a place
That I recall

As a child
On Grandpa's farm
A place to hide
Away from harm

This place I called
The Tunnel Trees
For that is how
They seemed to me

The pathway
Underneath them long
The branches stretching
Oh so strong

It's here that I
Would go to play
On every sort
Of different day

In Summer, shade
Beneath the leaves
I'd scarcely see
The branches weave

In Winter, snow
Would cover thick
The branches seemed
Like stark, dead sticks

In Spring, new life
Began to show
With happiness
My soul would grow

In Fall, bright colors
Drift on the air
Until the branches
Were quite bare

And so I'd play,
I'd gaze, I'd think
Beneath kind natures
Timely link

Grandma had a tiny sewing room right off the corner of the family room and I was seldom allowed inside. She thought I'd mess things up and that may have been true; I didn't really care to spend my time inside anyway. It was the outdoors that truly intrigued me. Every space in that house had some sort of use and everything was always in it's place. Every hallway had drawers and every drawer had it's special purpose and you were allowed to touch things if you could put them away, <u>exactly</u> as you'd found them. Even the 1/4" dice had to be perfectly stored. I never gave it much thought until recently; that attention to detail was all Grandma. I somehow landed with the same structure that she had, although I've only come to realize it recently upon traveling to see Stony Creek, Connecticut, were it is said, she was born. Several years ago I searched back into our genealogy as I had questions about where we had come from and how we got to California when so many of our relatives had lived back east.

My mother's side came directly from Ireland and my husband and I took a trip a few years ago to meet family members in Northern Ireland, in the county of Antrim. It was there that I found a cousin who I have a very familiar resemblance to. He too, is quiet and unassuming and loves the outdoors. He made a living spending much of his adult years surveying the parks and waterways. In those photographs we took, I can see a resemblance that looks as if we are very much connected. I found that my other relatives there seemed to share my fascination for cows. They are dairy farmers and breed specialty cows and bulls. I doubt that they sing to their cows as I did as a child, but they fully understand a good cow from a bad one and didn't even want me to take photos of those cows they found unfit. I thought this one cow's curly hair was mesmerizing, but they would hear nothing of it, he wasn't a cow that was a worthy, well bred example of one of their cows. We had a wonderful time touring the countryside, although, as we hurriedly toured it, it seemed that we rarely stopped for even the tiniest of trinkets. This is why my husband and I are compelled to return again someday. We'll return, certainly for souvenirs, but also to see the family again. They are lovely people. Our trip was too short, indeed. Ireland is a lovely country and our time there was spent in splendid sunlight and rolling green hills. They say they never have weather like that, but indeed they do. We soaked up every bit of it, as never a raindrop fell. It is here that I thought my journey could end in the search to find someone who was somewhat like me.

Looking left to right in the above photo are: Bonnie (myself), my husband John, Margaret (my second cousin's wife), and my second cousin John. This was taken during a lovely walk at Whitehead in County Antrim, Northern Ireland.

Flower Garden

A couple of years passed and I still found that I continued to have a certain curiosity about Stony Creek. I've always thought that it is a lovely name to give a town. I thought it must be a wonderful place. My grandma didn't seem like she had come from a lovely place. Her life seemed complicated and hard to me. My grandparents weren't people that you would spend quality, fun time with as a kid. There were always clothes to be hung on the line outside that ran through the middle of the rhubarb garden, or dishes to be washed, or plants to be watered by hand. There must have been sprinkler systems but I can't remember my grandparents having that sort of time saving device at their finger tips. It seems that I have a recollection that Grandpa did finally get a sprinkler that would attach to the end of the hose and slowly rotate back and forth. I'm sure that saved them considerable time. My grandmother's favorite flowers were tall carnations, sweet peas, tall plate sized dahlia's, continuous begonia's, and hanging fuchsia's. Grandma had hanging fuchsias outside the corner of her kitchen. Those deep crimson and purple blossoms would hang down, and I knew I wasn't supposed to touch them but they were irresistible to me. I'd reach as high as I could and ever so gently squeeze the edges of the blossom ball, and, "pop," it would open. It made a wonderfully delightful sound. I didn't see anything wrong with it, I was just giving the blossom a little help in opening. Well, sure enough, the next time Grandma would see me at her home, the first thing she would say to me would be, "I don't want you popping my fuchsias." She then would simply walk away. I could never figure out how she knew that I had, indeed, popped those blossoms. I would always carefully peek in the kitchen windows to make sure she wasn't watching, before I'd touch any of her blossoms. I never figured it out until years later when I grew some hanging fuchsias of my own, and had children of my own, just how Grandma always knew what I was up to. I popped a couple of my own blossom balls and returned the following day. It seems those flowers are not ready to pop until they do it on their own. Upon checking on them the next day I found the edges of the blossoms to be brown and not nearly as pretty as they would have been, had I left them alone. So Grandma wasn't psychic, she was disappointed in the results she was seeing in the blooms and of course in me, who wasn't listening to her and following her wishes. I had popped those blossoms of mine so I could know when my children were playing with my fuchsias. Oddly enough, they never did. I never told them not to, and they never touched them. I don't know if that was because I hadn't brought it to their attention or if they simply weren't interested in those flowers. I have a grandchild myself now, who is very much like how I was as a child. Maybe she will be out popping the fuchsias. If she does, I'll show her what the results are of her impatience and I doubt she'll not find a way to wait a little while longer for the beautiful flower. This is a tiny lesson that can be well taught by a grandmother. I had to find the lesson on my own; I guess that was my grandmother's way of teaching me. I now wonder if my grandmother was a fuchsia popping little girl in her own right. I often wonder too, if I fully grasped the lessons that she may have been trying to teach me.

Inside my grandparent's house were wood and linoleum floors and on these floors were braided rag rugs that my grandmother had compiled by hand for her family. She did a wonderful job on these rugs and it wasn't until her passing that I even knew that she had made these, herself. Some of them were very large and some small enough to rest beneath the sink in the kitchen. The rest of the family members had no attachment to those old rugs and were happy to part with them upon my grandfather's passing, a few years later. They parted with a lot of very important things, the jigsaw puzzles, the rugs, the two family bibles (imagine; thank goodness my mother had the sense to at least, remove the front pages and photo copy the family registers from both of the bibles), and the paint-by-numbers. I know we can't keep everything forever but one jigsaw puzzle, one rug, the one and only, tattered black leather, family bible dating back to 1834, and one of the best of the paint-by-number paintings all placed neatly in a box, tupperware tub, or large, well marked, baggy would have been a nice touch for future generations. I guess they never thought we'd be curious, but curious I am, and the time to have my innumerable questions answered is surely coming to an end. The people with the answers are in their eighties now and some, not so sure minded any longer. I need to find access to these people so I can paint these pictures firmly in my mind; those I know to be true and verify those I think I remember. With all that being said, I am so very thankful for those things that have been saved and passed down over the generations.

Alice's Tongue

I entered my Grandma's kitchen one day and I must have been all of about eight years old. Grandma told me I could have a piece of horehound candy and I knew just where to find it in her pantry. I entered at one end and came out the other end and she told me that she wanted to show me what we were having for dinner. She told me to come closer. I think she wanted me to step away from the wood burning stove that stood at the end of the kitchen. She took a large fork and stabbed what was in the pot on the stove. Pulling it up, she asked me if I knew what was for dinner. I'd never seen anything like it. It was an unusual grayish brown color and was very long and bumpy. "What is that?" I asked. "Well, we're having cows tongue tonight," and she smiled at me. I remember thinking, why would you eat cow's tongue? At that moment a light went on in my head and I asked, "Is that Alice's tongue?" "Well yes it is, and I don't often get to cook cow's tongue," she replied. I am rather surprised, to this day that, that event didn't cause me to become a vegetarian, and it probably most certainly would today. I would have almost starved had I tried to do something like that during that course of my life, while residing at my parent's house. It never would have flown with my parents, as every meal we ever had was laced with some sort of meat. We were always required to finish every bite. I have lived my entire life eating what I like least first, and saving what I like best on my plate to eat last. Since becoming an adult, I do not eat every bite; I eat only until I'm satisfied with the individual selection I have chosen, making sure to leave enough room for whatever is my favorite on the plate. My husband thinks this is a crazy way to eat. I am quite satisfied eating this way. I think he eats way too fast and is often done before I have tried my second bit or section of food. He came from a very large family and you had to eat quickly so you might finish in time to get seconds. We both developed our eating practices early in life and find it very difficult to break them.

I refused to eat Alice's tongue that evening. I couldn't believe they would eat Alice! She was surely the finest cow I had ever known. What a sad, sad way for her to be used. All the adults knew what Alice was being raised for. I only knew that I loved her. She was a beautiful reddish color and oh so sweet, aren't all cows after all? She seemed happy to have me placed on her back and she never even mooed while they would lead her about with me singing joyously on her back. I am sure Alice was in the freezer at my mother's home but she never let on when dinner was, indeed, Alice. It does make sense that my father had acquired her from a local dairy and had brought her to my grandfather's place. She had been raised as a cow for consumption. My father and grandfather surely had been in on this conspiracy together.

Not too long ago I was given some copies of old poems that my great grandfather, who grew up in Connecticut, had written many years prior. This is my grandmother's father and I am not totally sure that she knew he wrote poetry. What interested me in this poem was the fact that, he too, seemed to have an interest in cows. The writing on the pages is faded but still very visible and the paper has yellowed over time. I have attempted to decipher what was written on each page and follow exactly what he wrote in the same manner that he wrote it.

When I Was A Boy

1

Not for years had I passed this way so on one crisp October day.
I gave Shanks Mare the reign and bid him travel oer again up and through fields now grey to scenes not seen for many a day.

2

The most natural thing in the world to do was to start at the barn and go right up through. The cow paths who's tortuous ways were precisely the same as in childhood days.

3

I cut a small while where the straightest ones grew and flicked off the head of a thistle or two. Thistles and daisies were once my game when my heart was light and yet untamed.

4

Just over the top of the hill to the right, the cows drinking and wallowing place came in sight. Brought plainly to view some strenuous times when my oft called Co Boss they as often declined.

5

The cows most always "twas meanness I know" at about milking time when the sun was low. Would patiently wander meanwhile chewing their cud and plant themselves down in two feet of mud.

6

Ten cows to one boy was no fair even match an we chased oer the swamp near the cranberry patch. Oer bog, oer stone, through mud and brier that job at least was worthy its hire.

7

Where beyond this point I'd occasionally roam where lost in my sights were the chimneys of home. Oh wondrous adventure the climax of joy to be almost lost was great fun for a boy.

8

Sometime when the frost had settled down and the north wind with nuts had strewn the ground. A dozen children more maybe, would go over the hill to the chestnut tree. And whither our luck was a peck or more we could tell fish stories when I was a boy.

9

There was naught in life that was not ours from the wooded hills to the garden flowers. Nothing now could be the same as around the ring in the marble game. We often owned air, land, and sea, when I was boy it seemed to me.

Wm. Goodhue Bates was my great grandfather's name. I have a photo of him sitting in a very large scrolled chair. He had a bald head and a long straight nose. Beneath that nose was a large handlebar mustache and a long go-tee that looked as if he combed it from the middle so it would brush out toward his ears. It's quite a unique look, I must say. He had written many poems and I've often wondered if he ever dreamt of being published.

Great Grands

In an attempt to confirm what I believe to be true in my mind, I spoke with my father, my sister, and my aunt. I would have loved to talk with my mother about her memories but they have faded, the long and the short of them all, I'm afraid. Grandma taught my mother how to make the perfect pie crust and she never taught any of her, three, daughters. My mother was still in her teens when she married my father and they moved in with Grandma and Grandpa. I am quite sure that my grandmother had a big influence in how my mother came to cook and bake things. Since my mother did not teach any of us the secrets of baking the perfect crust, I am afraid that art may be gone for good, as I make an excellent filling but purchase my crust, pre-made. My mother has always marveled at my pie fillings and it isn't really any novel thing that I do. I simply follow the recipe and whip a little longer or add an extra peach or two. I never thought much of my mother's pies as she would take the filling for one pie and use it for two. This means that pumpkin pies are very thin and dry and truly not good to eat, but I always loved eating the extra pieces of pie crust, sprinkled with cinnamon and sugar, that came warm from the oven. Mom loved me eating them too, as nothing would go to waste upon consumption.

A few years ago I borrowed my mother's cookbook (there was only one) and her limited recipe box in an attempt to put together a cookbook for my sisters that they could cherish. I did the scanning, and this is the recipe that is still idly sitting in my computer, patiently waiting for me to return to, a great idea, someday. Although that recipe book is still an incomplete project, here is the recipe my mother used to make a delightful pie crust.

Mother's Pie Crust
Sift together:
4 C flour
4 tsp. baking powder
2 tsp. salt

Mix well:
1 1/3 C shortening
1 C hot water
2 tbsp. lemon juice
2 egg yolks, unbeaten
Stir into flour mixture
Chill
Pat out 3/4 of the pastry in 8" pie dish.
Dot with bits of butter (1 tbsp per crust, prick bottom crust) and fill.
Cover with the rest of the pastry.
Bake at 425 for 25 min.

I believe this recipe to be doubled as I have a firm recollection that Mom always made 2 pies. I have not tried this recipe, but I think I must soon. The down side of this is that my husband won't want me to use pre-made pie crust again, if I can come anywhere close to duplicating my mother's pie crust. He thinks my mother made the best pie crust he has ever tasted. Please note that he liked her crust; he was also never a fan of her fillings.

In the quest to find my mother's recipes, I came across a hand written Tamale Pie recipe from my grandmother. She would have us over to dinner occasionally and was so very proud of her tamale pie. We couldn't stand it, but were always instructed to smile and tell her how very wonderful it was. What made Grandma's tamale pie so horrid was her, sometimes, doubling of the corn topping to make the pie go further. It made the whole thing just awful and chokingly dry. Here is Grandma's recipe exactly as she wrote it

Tamale Pie

Put to soak the night before 2 or 3 cups of pink beans.
In the morning cook beans until tender, pour off water and mash beans.
Cook about 1 or 2 lbs of beef in about 1 qt of water when tender remove meat from water and save water.
Grind meat in food grinder.
Cook until tender about (1 hr) 2 large onions and grind up also.
Cook about 4 red dried chili pepper, after they have been washed and cleaned of seeds, about 1/2 hr or until the meaty part can be scraped off from the skin.
Drain 1 qt of tomatoes.
Add pulp to other ingredients and save juice to drink.

Mix all together and season with a dash or two of Cayenne pepper, about 2 or 3 teaspoons of chili powder.
Salt to taste.
Measure meat water and add enough water to make 8 cups, salt, bring to boil.
Add slowly and stir constantly 2 cups sifted corn meal.
Cook until thick or about 5 minutes.
Put in layers in 2 large casseroles or several small ones.
Keep in refrigerator until ready for use.
Bake in moderate oven about an hour.
Serve hot.

While going through some of my grandmother's recipes, it was interesting to see how much lard was used and how often she would remind herself that she should do things like drinking the leftover tomato juice. I don't know if this came from the time she was a child or if the depression led her to have such practices. I often wonder how my grandmother came to have the kitchen practices that she did. Was it from her mother, or her grandmother? My grandma's mother and father had come to California around 1912. It appears that a lot, and new home, were purchased and built around 1915 on Benton Way in Silver Lake, California as there are photos that substantiate that. I've been told many times, by my father, that my grandmother had a major breakdown after her second child was born and I believe that her mother and grandmother felt it was important to move closer to her so they could be of help to my grandma. It appears that they didn't stay long on Benton Way. My grandma had three more children after the breakdown and her mother and grandmother continued to live very near my grandma until each of their passings. I have often wondered if her cooking skills were self taught, as mine surely are.

I remember my great grandmother, (Grandma's mother), Ida, and I also remember her funeral. I wrote about it, many years later, as it was a feeling that I didn't want to simply abandon.

Great Grandma Bates

I remember when you died
How I cried out loud inside
But no one shed a single tear
There I stood, so small, in fear

As I grew, I came to know
Why no one let their feelings show
Someday they would see you soon
Up among the clouds we'd loom

Something struck me strange one day
What if they were wrong, someway?
What if there were no tomorrow?
They had only hid their sorrow

That's the day I came to know
I would let my feelings show
Each day walk with head held high
And when in sorrow, I would cry

There is an incredibly sad event that happened in my family. Great Grandma Bates died in Santa Cruz and was buried down in Colton, California. I have discovered that her number on her gravesite is 4275. There has not been a marker with her name on it for 50 years. What causes a family to never put the final touches to a loved one's resting place? They didn't cry when she died at 91. I wanted to, but no one cried. Was she a horrible person? Were her children fighting over who should pay for the headstone? I'll pay for the headstone! It just isn't right. It embarrasses me that this task was never completed. I'll not only pay for the headstone, but if I can, it's going to be done in Stony Creek pink granite. That is a fitting stone to represent her, and be placed on her gravesite. She lived there and a piece of the place should remain with her. Those people who were responsible for this are long gone now, and we as a family should have made this right long ago. Sometimes it's best to put your feelings aside and just follow through and do the right thing.

I've recently been sent the final proof for the marker. It was difficult for me to find the proper words that would have fit her. I was only six when she died. I simply tried to sum up her life. I placed this on her marker:

Ida Mae Chidsey-Bates
Stony Creek, CT Feb. 23, 1871
Santa Cruz, CA Mar. 21, 1962
Daughter, Wife, Mother,
Grandmother, Great Grandma,
Simple Love, Simple Life

We, as women, are often all of these things. Simple love was what I hoped she felt toward and from her family. I hope that love came easily for her. If you can find a simple love like that, than your life should be much more enjoyable and the choices that you make should come simply for you. The flowers that I had engraved on the pink granite marker are Mountain Laurels, and are Connecticut's state flower. They represent ambition and perseverance. She surely had both of those qualities. I am sure she enjoyed these each spring as I remember mention of them during her daughter's travels in 1954.

The Great Grand Adventure

On Sunday, May 16, 1954 at 5:45 p.m., (surely after a full day at the local church) my grandmother embarked on a train trip that would take her across the country, back to the places of her childhood. She was 58 and was traveling by herself. It was the first and last documented trip of this sort that she would take. I don't know how she talked my grandfather into letting her go, but clearly she did. She kept meticulous notes on her journey and it is clear to see, that as she crossed the United States, she was looking for something specific. Upon reading her three tiny spiral bond memo pads, where she wrote those notes, I believe she was looking for the familiar sights and smells of the wooded areas on the east coast. She kept these memories to share and she kept them for herself. They were safely tucked away in two old greeting card boxes that were labeled for easy retrieval. She snapped photographs and wrote on the back of each, describing the place and time or people in each picture and numbered on the top so they traveled, with each viewing, the same path as she had shot them. She also sent home post cards that she later retrieved to add to the numbered photos, each in it's proper place, all chronologically numbered to create her collection of memories.

I do much the same thing as she did when I travel. I am not limited to the film rolls of 12, 24, or 36 photographs as in the past. I can, not only see the result of my photo on the camera, but I am free to shoot hundreds of photos as I travel, and indeed I do. I come home, select my favorites, print, post, and label in a photo book within three days of returning home from my travels. It sounds a bit as if I've got obsessive compulsive disorder, but this habit has proven to be quite beneficial when friends want to talk about my most recent trip. It can be helpful too, when I'm asked about places that I've visited when a friend is embarking on a similar trip of their own. It's been a precise and wonderful way to help refresh my memories of some of my favorite places that I've seen. My family doesn't seem interested in the diaries that I keep on my travels, which is very interesting to me. I do not think that any of my grandmother's family has ever taken the time to look at these journals and photos that she held so dear. It took me 50 years to find them myself, and it was only after I had traveled to Stony Creek,

Connecticut that I have fully accessed them. I will return again, as I now have a better sense of her time there in 1954. I often wonder when the time will come that one or all of my children will want to wrap up in a cozy blanket and hangout on a couch to read my travel diaries, view my photo books, and get to know me a little better. Unfortunately I'll probably be long gone and unable to fill them in on those truly delightful times. I have many travel journals and photos so it may prove to be a daunting task. Perhaps they will pick certain places of interest to them, for their viewing.

As Grandma journeyed, from Pomona, California on the train, she was always pleased to have a window seat so she could review all that she was seeing. Her first stop was Las Vegas, Nevada and on to Salt Lake City, Utah where the passengers changed and there were new people to talk with. I never knew my grandmother to be outgoing, but I can see her interest in the people that she met on the train. She stopped at Green River, Utah to purchase stamps so she could stay in touch with all those she had left behind and perhaps also to stay in touch with the people she was traveling to meet. There were no cell phones back in 1954; she was on her own. She was looking out the window and noticing the farms, the "bright full moon," and undoubtedly dreaming about the people she was going to reunite with. She noticed more farms by Cheyenne, Wyoming and into Nebraska but she thought Iowa was, "beautiful farming country." The train crossed the Mississippi at Clinton, Iowa and from there it was two more hours to Chicago, Illinois; her first destination point on the trip. Her arrival in Chicago was on time and she took a Parmelee Transfer Cab to the Burlington Line, lunched at Pennsylvania Station and bought a ticket to Aurora, Illinois. She was going to Aurora to visit Marie and Gerald (Jerry) Richardson and spend the night. Marie picked her up and drove her by their church on the way to a mother daughter banquet that was being held at the YMCA cafeteria. She thought it was very nice and I'm sure she must have reflected on what it would have been like to share events like that with her daughter, had she not passed away. She met many of the faculty at the college and found the city of Aurora to be, "tree filled with tulips and lilac everywhere." Marie had a bouquet of Lily of the Valley waiting in her room. She so loved that thoughtful touch. She was off on her journey early the next morning with a cab ride to the Central Station. On this ride she noticed that many of the houses were made of brick. She notices that they are, "passing through a woody place with streams of water and ponds and there is one pond covered with water lilies, which reminds her of the quarry in Stony Creek, Connecticut." (I wish I knew which quarry that was.) She commented that this train, that she was on, was not nice like the Union Pacific and there were many people smoking on the train. She thought that she would be, "well scented," by the time she reached her destination. But with that being noted, she turns her eyes to, "the beautiful lakes," when entering Ann Arbor, Michigan and, "the green rolling hills, the shining sun with white clouds and the brisk breeze." I find her to be drinking up all that she can visually.

Grandma is on this train, to Detroit, to visit her Uncle Will Chidsey. She noticed that while going through Cedar Rapids, Iowa that there were no railroad crossing gates only a man with a small stop sign to alert drivers of oncoming trains. She also noticed that all the big barns and houses had lightening rods on them. She thought the Illinois scenery was much like that of Iowa. Upon arriving in Detroit, someone named Bill and Clara meet her and take her sight seeing and I am guessing they are related to Uncle Will but she makes little mention of ever seeing her uncle. Upon reading her notes again, and spending hours of deciphering on a favorite genealogy site, it seems to me that Uncle Will is indeed Bill, and she has become more familiar with him and his wife and so readily, refers to them in less formal terms.

She travels through Palmer Park and Palmer Wood onto Outer Drive through Rouge Park where there are lovely homes. They traveled through the tunnel under the Detroit River and came out in Windsor, Ontario Canada where she stops to buy trinkets for her grandchildren back home. They head back over the Ambassador Bridge then to Belle Isle and around to Lake Shore Drive by Lake Sinclair and up to Birmingham where she stops again to send a telegram to Bessie to notify her of her arrival on Monday the 24th of May. She visits with a friend who's name is Mena, and goes for a walk in the woods with her where she finds wild violets, yellow violets, and ferns. She sees Walled, Upper Straights, Orchard, Pine, Keego Harbor, the new Northland Shopping Center all before continuing her train journey on, "The Wolverine," to Detroit, Michigan and New York. The train stops at St. Thomas, Canada, Buffalo, New York, Fort Erie, Black Rock, and Syracuse. While passing through Utica, New York she notices, "green rolling hills and the sky is covered with little clouds and it looks like rain," to her. She remembers that a sky like that used to be called, "a Mackerel Sky." In Schenectady, New York she sees only lilacs and lovely tulips. Upon entering Albany the conductor starts calling the station names and there is now food service available.

Quandaries

Stony Creek is a beautiful little village on the Long Island Sound. I can only imagine how difficult it must have been to leave such a place to move west to a new and unknown place. Certainly the weather of California was a definite draw but I understand that grandma's father had noises in his head that his physician thought might be helped by a drier climate. You can't get much drier them ultimately living in Banning, as it is on the way to Palm Springs which has a very arid climate. They did, however, first move to Riverside County in California. Great Grandpa's voices never did recede until he opted for surgery in 1939 to relieve the sounds that plagued him. He acquired phenomena, during his recovery from that surgery, and the sounds in his head permanently ceased, as he passed away from that illness. They had been in California for twenty-seven years before Great Grandpa had that surgery done. Was the move away from family and friends worth such a life altering decision? It is hard to say, but I would not be here today if that cross country move had not taken place, as Grandma never would have met my grandfather and her life undoubtedly would have been quite different. My grandparents were not warm, loving people. My aunt uses the word austere to describe them. The problem with being stern and closed off is that it filters down to your offspring and down to their offspring and so on and so forth until someone puts a halt to the loneliness that surrounds this joyless, ultra structured, nearly mechanical existence. I do not believe that my grandmother was truly the person we all perceived her to be. She was educated, kind, thrill seeking, loving, and desiring of finding the beauty that visually surrounded her. Even while on her trip, she united with a friend and was busy sewing her a dress while on vacation. What drives a person to spend their time doing that? Was she seeking the approval of her friend? Was she unable to ever sit idly still? Did she want to try to make sure her friend would remember her once she had returned home? Was she trying to feel better about her travels away from family? These questions, I'll never have answers to, but they make me look inwardly to try to find a better me. I needn't be complicated to people in my life. I need to be authentic and simply, me.

Why do we put up walls around us? What is it we think others will find so distasteful about us? I find it so very important to learn from those who have gone before us. We needn't make the same mistakes as others. I listen too much and laugh too little. I find a lack of authenticity in people, and they perhaps in me. This is not what I wish to portray. I am thoughtful and loving yet never wanting to be the fool. That foolishness is my downfall. I must learn to laugh at foolishness and embrace it. For me, that is easier said than done. We are always, a constant work in progress.

Grandma's shoes were nearly always black leather, and laced up. In the spring they looked exactly the same but in their white version. Upon asking my father about my memories of her shoes, I came to find that she had fallen arches and spent a lot of money on those shoes. I believe they were from a line of shoes called Enna Jettick Shoes Inc. The particular shoes that she wore, were truly the style for sensible women of the day. My other grandmother, who had immigrated from Northern Ireland, lived in Los Angeles, California and had shoes that very much resembled the ones I had grown accustomed to seeing my grandma Lewis in, who lived just across town. They were stable, as were those women. When I was young, I just imagined that all old ladies wore shoes like that. When you're young, you never dream that, you too, might someday be rethinking the usefulness of a practical, comfortable shoe. Does my granddaughter think that I wear old lady shoes? I don't perceive them that way, and they look nothing like my grandmothers shoes, yet I must always remember those feelings that are only a short memory away, so I can tune into youths thoughts and passions. Oh those splendid youthful thoughts. As you age, you find yourself growing fonder of those memories that your acquired in your youth.

I didn't realize how little I knew about my grandmother. I didn't realize how much I am like her. I didn't know that I could be like her and share her interests even though she seemingly didn't attempt to share herself with me. There is so much I feel that I can share with my grandchildren and so much I feel I need to show them. Could it be that they are born with a lot of me already inside of them? I hope they acquire all the best parts. Maybe that is why I am in their lives, to help discover and bring out the best parts of them; well, and then, they will bring out the best parts in me too.

It is always so very interesting to find that you possess qualities of people who were a relation to you. It is also unfortunate that we often discover those likenesses after that relation may have passed away. It is essential that we query those people around us and absorb all they have to offer while we are still developing ourselves.

Return to Stony Creek

As my grandmother entered Connecticut, she noticed that, "the Bridle Wreath was in bloom," and I can only imagine that this was one of those familiar sights that she had been looking for on her journey. Ernest and Bessie were in New Haven, Connecticut to meet the train and she makes mention in a large square box, while jotting down her notes, that she, "met a man on Uncle Timmy's place, his name was DeMattio." (Is her spelling of this name correct? I am not sure how this correlates to anything that she has written so far. It looks as if it was hastily jotted down on the page.) Ernest and Bessie took my grandma to see someone named Roger and his wife and she noted that, "he looked the same but his hair was white." She noted this about everybody and she even noted that about herself. They stopped in Short Beach at Bessie's, Aunt Cathy's place and proceeded on to Stony Creek. "The railroad station was gone but the road was still there," (and I think this was in reference to the trolleys that used to bring people to the beach). "The post office was the same in 1954 as she had remembered, as was the store below it. They came near the 3 stores together near where Captain Cooper had lived and then the stone church was there." (I saw that stone church when I was there. It is made of the pink granite that Stony Creek was famous for).

When I was in Stony Creek, I was amazed to find out how many monuments, that I had seen on our travels, were made of the local pink granite. Monuments like The Lincoln Memorial, Grant's Tomb, The Statue of Liberty, The Battle Monument at West Point (and it is mentioned in the family notes that Elbert Coe (Grandma's great grandfather) had somethng to do with that all coming to be, but I've had a difficult time confirming that), The Soldiers Monument, William Taft's Tombstone, The Soldiers & Sailors Monument in Albany, New York, and The Mother Goose Monument in Central Park, New York. Those just scratch the surface of the places that Stony Creek granite plays a prominent place in American monument making.

My grandma, Ruth, and her childhood friend, Bessie, stopped just beyond the Three Elm House and walked up the side road. "The hotel was there but the Elm trees had been cut down and the stumps left." I believe that my great-great grandmother helped run the Three Elm House. Her name was Harriet (Hattie) Coe Chidsey and she came west with my great grandmother and great grandfather, my grandma, and my grandma's brother. I have found that the house of Elbert Coe is a historical landmark and will do more to discover the facts about where that is placed.

As my grandmother continued on with her descriptions of her travels, she mentions that, "The old dance hall was still there and the old home place had not changed much but was now covered with asbestos shingles and the 2 porches looked wider and on the ground floor." (I do so wish she had taken down the addresses for those of us who came after). "There was a double garage under the porch. The old cherry tree was still there and the fence was down. The front was a little shorter as they had widened the street. Across the street the old store had been built onto and across the street from the store, by the water, was now a place to build boats. The swimming place was still there and the slid was there, perhaps to launch boats. The swanky hotel down-by the landing was not well kept up. The boat landing was now three instead of one. There were several boats docked there but none of them looked like public boats. The two nearest islands did not have houses on them but she could see that houses had once been there. Bessie thought maybe the hurricane of 1938 had taken them. Aunt Nay's house looked the same but no longer had a front porch. The store building had brown shingles and looked more like a house then it used to. She thought there was a bay window in front. She went down to what was Uncle Timmy's house but it was private now." (I believe this was the place she was referring to when meeting Mr. DeMattio.) She saw a man working and asked, "if she could take a picture or 2 and introduced herself. He knew Uncle Timmy, The Coe's, and The Chidsey's. She thought he was very nice. She went down to the point which was mostly private too. She was going to buy oysters or clams but the place was not open so she went to what she called, "Grandma's Store" and bought 2 lobsters to take to Camp Bethel." She later commented on how, "very good they were." I never knew my grandma to eat shell fish or any fish like that, and those 2 lobsters were not the end of her fish eating, during this excursion. She had fried clams twice, scallops, salmon, finnan haddie (a Scotland haddock), and her friend fixed, "delightful duck," for one of their dinners. This is a woman who, I knew as, cooking cows tongue! I am a lover of good food and obviously so was my grandma. Between moving west, meeting my grandfather, the depression, etc. she had lowered her standards for food consumption. All bets were off on this trip, and I can see that she was delighted in all of the culinary choices she was making. I wonder if she ever told Grandpa how much she splurged? I'm taking a look at her precise logs to see if she revealed everything......not that anyone was interested or looking to see what her travels had been.

This is a photo of my grandma on her trip in 1954. She had climbed out on this rock to have a picture taken of herself by her friends, Ernest & Bessie Whitney, at Chapman Falls and Devils Hopyard on the way to Camp Bethel in East Haddam, Connecticut. Note the shoes she was wearing. Those are the shoes that I remember my grandma wearing, every time that I saw her. It is obvious that she could get about quite nicely in them. We might refer to them as a sturdy multipurpose shoe today.

These are some of the detailed notes that she kept while on her trip. I am so interested in the price of some of the items. Two lobsters on May 24, 1954 were just $1.92, a clam dinner was $1.20, her cross country train fare was $158.25, and her largest splurge was a gold signet ring for my grandfather of $19.59 from Hulls Jewelry Store in Wallingford, Connecticut. That must have been some ring. I think that I vaguely remember it with his initial "R" on it. It was gold and black and I didn't see it very often. There must have been some very special candy later on in the trip when she reached Charleston, West Virginia because it was more expensive then all the other candy that she purchased and she returned twice for it.

Beyond being giving to my grandfather, it seems that the Lord had a very special place in her heart. I found another page of notes that I found fascinating. She would often give a dollar here and a dollar there for the Lord's work. It appears that she was especially moved a couple of times and gave three and five dollars upon hearing selected sermons. She wrote about those sermons in her notes, quite extensively. She also remembered her grandchildren, friends, and family and kept a list of those expenses as well, and also kept a list of where it was that she had stopped to purchase each of these gifts along the way. It seems that the place of purchase was almost more important to her than the item or the price.

I knew my grandma as a very private person and so I am wondering why she made the list of clothing she was washing and hanging on the line. I found this bit of information a charming piece of irrelevant nonsense, but she must have written it because she didn't want someone to think she was being lazy. I really don't know, but it made me giggle and go back and reread it as I thought I must have missed a line or two. It was almost more like a packing list then a laundry list. Perhaps that was it; it became her packing list. I do believe that people used to make laundry lists (what we call, "to do" or "honey do," lists today) in their everyday lives.

She had started the trip with $365.00 (a dollar saved each day for a year) and spent $345.46 not leaving her with a lot of extra change should any issue arise. Those were not the days of credit cards and cell phones, should there be a problem. She had $19.54 in her pocket when she returned home. I find that ironic, I wonder if she did too. She must have undoubtedly counted the remaining change and found that it was the same as the year, 1954, when she had taken the trip she so desperately wanted to go on. I understand that, in life, she was the one who always kept track of the family money, and so I guess her record keeping was just an extension of who and what she was destined to do. I am not like her in that respect. I do not know what a half gallon of milk costs or a gallon of gas. I am going to make my purchase anyway; so why fret about it? I am not, like her in that way because the world we live in today is oh so different from the world that my grandma lived in.

White Sapphires

W hen the family decided to pack up and move to California, my grandma's brother had a girlfriend. My great grandmother, Ida, thought he shouldn't leave her behind because it was, "the best he'd ever do." So they loaded the family onto a train that was bound for Ontario, Canada (or as they put it, Niagara Falls) and they were wed on October the 8th 1912. I am not sure how long it took the family to travel across the country, though we do have a photo of the newlyweds in El Paso, Texas on Oct. 20, 1912. It was an adventure, for sure. It was late in 1912 that the family left, collectively, to California. I believe my great-great grandmother moved from Connecticut to California, a few years later, about 1915, as I have a photo, dated 1915, of my great-great grandmother, Harriet Coe Chidsey, and her sister, Nellie, in Niagara Falls and it is clearly marked on the photo that they were on their way to California. Hattie had decided to move to California and Nellie was traveling with her to visit with my grandmother and her new grandnephew. My grandma, Ruth, had moved west in 1912 with her mother, father, and brother (and of course her new sister-in-law). They moved to Colton, Riverside County, California. My grandma's father, Wm. Goodhue Bates, had worked for many years at the Wallace Silver plant on the Quinnipiac River in Wallingford, Connecticut. Since he had developed noises in his head, the family moved to the drier climate in California, with the hope that it would bring him relief. I believe he had Tinnitus for more than 30 years of his life. I believe my grandma was about 17 when they moved. I am sure there were many letters back to Connecticut to tell everyone about the weather in California and eventually my great-great grandmother decided to come west too. Harriet (Hattie) had been a widow for many years as her husband had passed away in 1896. She was only 48 at the time of his death and I can only imagine that it was a very hard life back in Cheshire and Stony Creek for an aging widowed woman at that time. I often wonder how women survived without social security, pensions, medicare, etc. I think families were close and extended, and as a community, they cared for one another.

Not terribly long after my grandma, Ruth, arrived in California, she met my grandfather. It may have been while attending an Advent Christian tent meeting, or working at the Colton Hardware Company, or perhaps simply attending the same church. I suppose it doesn't matter so much how they met, as the reality is that they did indeed meet and somehow struck a fancy for each other. The story is told that Grandpa had a real liking for my grandma. (It's actually funny for me to think of it in these terms because, when you are young and finding love, the last thing you have on your mind is eventually becoming someone's grandparent.) My grandfather, Ray Lewis, had arrived in California from Kansas with his mother, one brother, and two sisters. They were coming to California with his mother's family for work, as my grandfather was in the 8th grade when his father had left the family for a pianist in town. My grandfather, being the eldest, had left school to help his mother provide for his siblings. I can not fully explain how this turn of events impacted my grandfather. I think that he felt cheated in life by this and it left him bitter and unforgiving at times. His mother had two brothers who were builders. They were relocating to California and suggested that the family come along. The brothers eventually settled in the Stockton, Modesto, Lodi area. His mother's name was Jennie Mary Hibbard (Lewis) and I am told that she was a lovely lady.

The story is told that, my grandfather asked my grandma to marry him three times before she conceded. It is said that my grandma was way out of his league, but then again, he'd figured out a way to reach her. They were married in 1914. Their first child was born in 1915 and my father, as the youngest, came along about nine years later. It was somewhere in that time-frame, and an additional three children later, that my grandma took her diamond ring to the jewelers to have it cleaned. She was crushed to find out that her diamond was, "the nicest white sapphire I've ever seen," as she was told by the jeweler. Well, that didn't sit well with Grandma, who I'm sure felt duped at the time, and she came home and never wore that ring again. I remember her wearing a simple, yet thick, gold band as her wedding ring. I have been interested in that white sapphire ring for years but am afraid it was given away or even thrown away. See here's the problem, she felt that he had lied to her from the very beginning of their relationship. There she was, four or five children later, and what was she to do? Certainly she was very upset with him, but there are times in any marriage where you just have to move on and get over your discrepancies. None of us should live with the frustrations of the past, constantly playing over in our mind. I can not tell you how very important the person that you marry, is for you. You not only marry that person but their entire family too. If it looks like there could be serious problems ahead, then run for the hills. You are better off relying on yourself then to be buried in a bad marriage and lose your sense of self. I am so very happy that Grandma found her sense of self and took that adventure back to Connecticut and West Virginia.

With the white sapphire story, running through my head, there came a time, not too long ago, when my father had me fix a ring for my mother and he had me put a white sapphire in it for her. My mother, Nancy, being short on memory, somehow dropped her wedding ring down the garbage disposal, a few years ago, and ground it up a couple of times. We didn't do anything with it at the time as it had lost it's main diamond and looked as if, it may have been beyond repair. Mom had two other diamond rings and so it seemed unimportant to get that one fixed. In 2009, Dad had a 4th heart attack and they moved to a small house closer to town to help him get back on his feet. She had her jewelry there, and she always kept her jewelry box open and on the dresser. It's not the safest place for your jewelry, but she'd forget where she'd placed things and I guess that was a good place to remind her to wear her rings and things. She has always been a very trusting woman. Many people came and went in this house, and one day, her two diamond rings were missing.

It is sad for me to realize that there are people in this world that see surroundings like this as, "their lucky day," and never stop to think that it would produce, "the worst day ever," for the person they are violating. Nevertheless, we can't go back and recover those things taken and so we move on. It bothered Mom that she didn't have her ring, so I suggested to Dad that I might be able to get the old ring fixed through a jeweler in Graeagle, California. Dad thought it was a good idea, and I took the ring to the jeweler to see what he could do. I thought at the time that the ring would have to be melted down and reworked. I knew that it didn't have to be exactly as it had been, as she wouldn't truly remember. The difference in price between a diamond and a white sapphire was considerable and Dad thought she might just lose it again, so he opted for the white sapphire. He mentioned to her, a couple of times, that it wasn't a real diamond and she didn't seem to understand what he was saying. She was just happy to have her ring back and the jeweler did an outstanding job, on it's reconstruction. It looked exactly as it had when it was new. It is ironic to me that Grandma and Mom both had white sapphires, for a time, in their wedding rings. Mom is now in assisted care, as she's been diagnosed with dementia, and I can only hope that ring remains with her as, although it is a white sapphire, she still cherishes it.

Stairway to Heaven

W hen my grandma had her stroke, she spent a long period of time in a convalescent hospital. She was doing her rehabilitation there before they would release her to go back home. I doubt that she would have imagined what was about to happen to her, once she returned home. Grandfather decided that they should make some candy. Now given that she was virtually paralyzed on one side of her body, this would have been quite a fete. He propped her up on a stool and handed her the spoon so she could stir the hot liquid in front of her. Well, just about anyone could guess what might transpire. Grandma, lost her balance and fell off the stool and on to the floor. What happened next is the part that, I doubt, even she couldn't see coming. Grandfather proceeded to strike her multiple times, on her leg, with the burning hot, candy laden spoon. This put her back into the convalescent hospital and it was there that she begged my mother, her daughter-in-law, to make sure that she would remain there. She did not want to return to her home nor to her favorite lilac colored bedroom. She did indeed stay there; until her dying day. The only reason that I can tell this story is that I just happened onto the scene while visiting Grandma one day. The nurse came in to change her bandages and she asked me to exit the room and wait in the hall. My mother came by to visit while I was waiting and I asked her, "Why does Grandma have bandages that need changing?" My mother was very reluctant to tell me what had transpired and she wanted me to be silent about it. I was for many years, but it tells the story of our family. I struggled when writing this as it lets a family secret out that some might have thought would be better left unsaid. If it did stay silent and buried, would it help us all to understand where we came from? I think that family secrets can destroy a family and I found it so hard to imagine that my grandfather was in heaven for the longest time. He was sure he was going there, but I struggled with the thought that heaven would house people who behaved in this manner. I am older now and the world is such a violent place. Where is that defining line between good and evil? I am no man's judge. I do find it so sad that Grandpa couldn't find it in himself to have kindness and compassion for Grandma, especially since she had taken care of him for most of his adult life.

Just three years after Grandma passed away, my grandfather just couldn't get past her being gone; he would go on and on about how much he loved her. He checked himself into a convalescent hospital across town and I think he stopped eating and drinking, which led to his death. I went and visited him only once while he was there, as I lived a far distance away and was pregnant, with my first child, at the time. He wasn't there long. My father, who lived in the same town, never visited him while he was there. I haven't any ideas about why that was. Perhaps he knew what Grandfather was about to do. Maybe it was his way of protesting that act. Maybe he just didn't want to deal with it. Whatever his reasoning, I've never asked him about it and he's never confided in me as to his feelings, regarding both of his parents having passed on. I think it's quite defining when both of your parents are gone and you realize that you are now the elder statesman. I went to see my grandfather because I think it is important to see and say what you want or need to say, before someone passes away. Memorials are fine for support of the family members, but I do hope that those who love me, would come and spend a little quality time with me before I go. One would think that the story ends upon one's passing, but I have found that in many ways it begins again as questions arise and answers are pondered. The realities of life and death are odd that way.

It has been a long standing tradition on my father's side of the family to give much, if not all, of your worldly goods to the church upon your death. There have been instances of someone claiming to be from the church, or the perception of being needier then your family members, that have also led to gifts prior to passing away. Grandpa did just that as he gave his cottage, at the camp grounds, to the church. This next thought will be a leap for some, but I'm going to ask my question anyway. We can't seriously think that we can buy our way into heaven, can we? I firmly believe that we get to heaven via our deeds, not our money. This is why charitable gifts in the end won't work in stepping you towards heaven. I am not opposed to gifting and charity; I just think it should come from a place of true kindness and compassion. It should not come from a place of fearful anxiety. You ultimately may make your family feel as if they were not important in your life, by seemingly ignoring their contributions to the family. What kind of God would think that leaving nothing to your family could possibly be good? It leaves your family grappling with unanswered questions. Your family are the ones who have tried to keep the mood sweet for you, even when you appeared not to have their best interests in mind. (Well, at least that has been what has transpired in my extended family over the years.) Let's say your family hasn't been supportive and kept the mood sweet for you, then do whatever you please but please also consider that you might not have been the nicest person on the planet and that is why you feel the need to buy your way into the pearly gates. I believe that in the end, those of us with an unsettled spirit have the greatest fear of dying, and what may lie before us. As my father grew older, he gave more and more of his money to just about any religious organization that asked for it. It was well beyond the 10% that we are led to believe we should give. Once again, I never asked him about it, but I did ask him to keep those excess dollars in a bank account in-case he or Mom needed the funds. He could leave his money to whomever or whatever organization he wanted, upon both of their passings. I felt that it was their money, after-all, to do with as they pleased. He wouldn't give that thought any consideration at all. It was as if he needed to make sure that he had given enough before he might pass away. They went without necessities but gave excessively to these organizations. I don't fully understand it.

It is amazing to think that my parents have been with me, my entire life. I have not been with them for their entire lives and they have not been together for their entire lives, but children are with their parents for their entire life. I am the youngest of three girls and feel fortunate in many ways that my father, for some reason, can communicate more easily with me than with my sisters. I really haven't a clue why that is. I am five and nine years younger than my siblings and given those ideas that I have just shared with you, I have a shorter lifetime invested, then they do. It is so sad to see how my father treats my sisters and for that matter my mother too. I wish I had the magic set of words that could heal them. That is a different book and a story that I have come to find many of the answers to.

Orchestration

I can not begin to express how truly gratifying it is to see the old photos in those sepia tones and return to the area where they were taken and find that the properties have been cared for in the manner that the former architects had intended. Certainly, not all of the structures remain, given hurricanes, fires, the great depression, and the shear impact of the elements of the sea. Some of those that do remain; they are elegant and I believe my ancestors were elegant in their own right. They were extremely hard working, entrepreneurial, community minded Americans.

I am grateful for these photographs with those images from the past. I share them with you because, in each of our pasts, there were those who came before us that paved a better way for generations to come. They wanted us to thrive, really, truly, thrive. I have found that my American lineage hales from as far back as a birth at Yarmouth, Barnstable, Massachusetts in 1652 and the earliest of settlers. I wonder if they would be proud of the Americans that, individually and collectively, we have become. Today, and each day, should be a day of celebration, for who we are, and who we can still become.

In ones life you chart a course to become who we see ourselves as being. When we are young, it may be hard to know just who we are, yet with that said, some of us know from an early age and go about becoming who and what we desire. I've often wondered what that later course would be like, as my parents did not seem to think that my desires were at all important. They were important to me and so I struck out at eighteen and tried, in my early twenties, to find out who I was. I was interested in horticulture and psychology yet my parents thought those not good fields to go into. I reluctantly listened and should not have done so. Both those fields completely fit who I am. The orchestration of my life is mine and no one else's. I fully realize that I impact others with my decisions, and that fact, became completely evident once I had a child and ultimately three children of my own. My life was no longer my own. It was time to devote myself to my family. I have no regrets with this and could not have achieved the successes with my children, had I been working full time. I chose to teach piano part time and work my schedule around my children's activities. They thought I was taking time away from them, but I was home and accessible to them. This is how I chose to orchestrate my life and the life of those who I had brought into this world.

My great grandfather, Melvin, who left his family of five, when my grandfather was in the 8th grade, had a different kind of orchestration in mind. I understand that he was quite an accomplished violinist who played in the local orchestra. He owned a prominent jewelry store in Kansas, when he decided to leave his family to be with the local pianist in town. He even came to his ex-wife and wanted the family piano for his new love interest. (The answer was a resounding, "No.") It devastated his family and one would think that he lived happily ever after with Susan. Oddly enough, he moved to San Diego, California from Kansas in the same time period that his first family was moving to Southern California. I've often wondered if he wanted to be closer to his children. Almost all photographs of him and his ancestors have been destroyed, as far as I know. I understand the reasoning behind that sort of behavior, but it leaves quite a hole for someone like me who has so many questions about those who have gone before.

Melvin was also a jeweler while he lived in San Diego. He died in his car, one day, from a heart attack, right before the Great Depression. What a lucky guy he was. He surely had a profitable business during the roaring 20's and he missed the misery that was about to fall on the country. He never had to endure the reality of how his children felt about him; nor did he ever witness the fallout of his actions on the generations to come. One might call it orchestration, one might call it karma, or one might call it luck. What I know is this, the actions you take as a parent completely impact your children for years, if not generations, to come. He wished not to have the responsibilities of a family, and once he, "fished his wish," it appears that his family may have been the only thing he did want. I wonder what his last few moments were like in his car. What flashed before his eyes? It is something to think about, when deciding the fate of so many innocent souls that you claim to love. Divorce is a devastating thing, there's no way around it. It is not ever a decision to make lightly.

Letter to Stony Creek

I am in awe of the power of computers to link with people instantly and the ability to cut and paste. Those of us who wrote term papers on typewriters fully realize what a blessed machine computers are. My husband and I went to Stony Creek about one week before Hurricane Irene struck. It was nothing like the hurricane that struck in 1938 but it was very large, none the less. It took me a couple of years to write the following letter, but I had so many questions upon walking through Stony Creek that I needed answers to and my grandma's notebooks gave me even more things to query about. When my husband and I took photo copies to Stony Creek, we came upon an apartment building that seemed to be the only place that #3 Elm Street could be. We met a gentleman, tenant, who invited us up on the porch and shared with us, who might be most knowledgeable of the history of the town. Little did we realize, that we were sitting on the reconstructed porch of the Three Elm House. There had been a fire and the once, three story house, was now two stories in height and was now an apartment building. It was like I was drawn to this structure, but it didn't fit the picture that I held in my hand. It was here that I was told about the minister in town. The following is what I wrote to the local pastor: (I have changed his name on the following pages.)

** October 9, 2012

Dear R. J., I spoke with you today and am writing to you to see if you have some knowledge of the history of the people of Stony Creek. I had started this letter last evening and so I will add that part here. My husband and I traveled to Stony Creek the summer before last as I was curious about the place where my grandmother was born. I had a few photos that I had found and took copies of them with us. We had little time there and I realized, while at the library, that I could only make a small dent in the information that I wanted to unveil. We did spend some time with a gentleman at 3 Elm Street. I think my great-great grandmother may have had some relationship to the Three Elm House. I have since gone through a diary that my grandmother compiled while on a visit to Stony Creek in 1954. The gentleman at 3 Elm said that you were very familiar with the history of Stony

Creek. We did come by the church but found no one there. I'm wondering if you can help me unravel some of the history that I am missing. I believe the Coe's and the Chidsey's were once quite well known in the town. I also have a photo that my grandmother marked as the place where her mother was born. The family had a direct link in Wallingford and my husband and I went there also but it was even a shorter visit than the one to Stony Creek. While in Stony Creek we did go out on the Thimble Island Cruise and saw a very familiar home that had been completely torn down and restored to it's original form. I think the Elbert Coe house has been placed on the historical list but I haven't any idea which house that might be. I am Bonnie DiMichele, my grandmother was Ruth Chidsey Bates (Lewis) who's parents were Ida Mae Chidsey (Bates), said to be born in Stony Creek, and Wm. Goodhue Bates. My great grandmother's parents were Lembert Chidsey and Harriet Coe (Chidsey) who, I believe, were active in Stony Creek and thought to be Masons. Lembert's parents died and he was raised by his Uncle Samuel Rose and Rebecca Rose. My great-great grandmother's parents were Elbert Coe and Louisa Bailey (Coe). I am under the impression that Elbert Coe owned a quarry in Stony Creek that made the large shaft for West Point.

The children of Elbert and Louisa Coe were, Ida Mae, Nellie, Harriet, Phoebe, and Timothy. I have one document that places them in Stony Creek in 1912. I believe Harriet and Nellie were quite close, and that Phoebe married into the Foote family. In 1954 my grandmother went to the Foote candy and ice cream store several times while visiting Wallingford, CT. Other names I have run across while looking through the documentation are Davenport, Bristol, Hooker, and Doolittle. In the 1880 census I have found Lembert R. Chidsey in Branford, New Haven, Conn. listed as an oysterman with wife Harriet M., children Ida M. (my great grandmother), George R., Edward S., and Ethel M. While reading the book Flesh and Stone, that I purchased at the library, I came upon some photos that looked like the old family photos that I have. This is why I am so curious about my family and Stony Creek. You reside in an absolutely gorgeous place, but I would guess that you are already well aware of the beauty that surounds you. I know that returning to Stony Creek in 1954 was very important to my grandmother and I believe that she compiled her notes and photos so she could relive that trip over and over again. I hope that you have a copy of Flesh and Stone as I will refer to it from time to time. I do not have many photos of Stony Creek that my grandmother took but the one's I do have leave me with questions, as does her description of her return to Stony Creek. We found the house that my great-great grandmother is standing in front of while in Stony Creek. I took photos and made note of the address but when I look in Flesh and Stone it says it is the Lundquist house on page 166 but I believe that is Harriet Coe (Chidsey) standing in front of that same house with a child at her feet. I don't know how it ties together. This house is on the corner of Thimble Island

Rd and Long Point Rd. On page 126 there is reference made to the West Point monument but it fails to say the name of the quarry that it came from. On page 65 there is a photo of Rand Point Coe's Dock on Long Point Rd. but even the book doesn't seem to know how the dock was used. I'm not positive that my grandmother wasn't born in that house that sits at the front of the dock. On page 81 there is a photo of Antonio Lazzari, the constable and I think he is in a photo with my grandmother with the rail tracks beneath them. You know Stony Creek better than I and I am about to write down what my grandmother said as she passed through town in 1954. Maybe you can visualize what she was seeing and were she was going. I'd love to return someday and have a better understanding next time I'm there. ** (The following is exactly as my grandma wrote it in her diary and may seem a bit repetitive but I wanted to create a flowing picture of what my grandma saw as she passed through town.)

Monday May 24, 1954...."Well I am in Conn. now. Just stopped at Stamford and I thought of Noni Gamble, as that is her folks home. The names the Conductor calls out sound familiar. Am glad they do not allow smoking. I feel like a smudge pot already. Now we are at Norwalk. This is truly a lovely country there are trees everywhere and it is not too flat. Just got my first glimpse of the Long Island Sound. Just saw some Dogwood trees. Mina had one but it was very small. The bridle wreath is in bloom also. Bridgeport is next. Quite a town. The clouds are forming into larger white ones showing blue through. It seems strange that people are carrying umbrellas. Just passed the large Singer Sewing Machine factory and many other familiar names. New Haven is next. Ernest and Bessie were there to meet me and we had lunch in the station and picked up my suit case. They took me to see Roger and his wife. He looks just the same as he used to but his hair was quite white. Then we stopped at Bessie's Aunt Cathy's in Short Beach from there we went to Stony Creek. The R.R. Station was not there but the road was. The Post Office was the same and the store below it. Then as we got near the 3 stores together near where Captain Cooper lived was just as it was. Then the stone church was the same. We stopped just beyond the 3 Elm house & Bessie and I walked up the side road. The hotel was there but the 3 Elm trees had been cut down and the stumps left but the porch did not come out to them. The old dance hall was still there and the old home place was not changed much, it was covered with asbestos shingles and the 2 porches looked wider and on the ground floor there was a double garage under the porch. The old cherry tree was still there and the fence was down. The front was a little shorter as they had widened the street. Across the street the old store building was still there and had been built on to. Across the street from the store by the water is now a place to build boats the swimming place was still there and a slid was there. I suppose to launch the boats. The swanky hotel down by the boat landing was there but not kept up very well. The boat landing had 3 landings instead of one. There were several boats docked there but none of them looked like public boats. The two nearest islands did not have houses on them but one could see that there had been. Bessie said maybe the hurricane took them. Aunt Nay's houses looked the same but they had no front porch and the store building had brown shingles and looked more like a house than it used too. I believe there was a bay window in front. Went down to Uncle Timmy's house and it was private road. I saw a man working around so I asked him if I could take a picture or 2. I introduced myself. His name was DeMattio. He knew Uncle Timmy and the Coe's and the Chidsey's. He seemed very nice. Then down to the point which was mostly private road too. Was going to buy oysters or clams but they were not opened so went back next door to Grandma's store and bought 2 lobsters (all they had). Then we drove to Camp Bethel cooked the lobster for supper and it was good." ** I will try to give the details that are located on the back of the photos that she took. My grandmother lived a very hard yet simple life. I never knew her as a person who loved lobster. I love lobster and did not develop a taste for it from my family as my grandmother had. While reading her travel book, I've come to find that my grandmother and I have much more in common then I had ever imagined. I'd love to know more, if you have the time. I see that you are retiring soon and I don't want to bother you, but it could be a fun diversion for you also.

Sincerely,

Bonnie DiMichele **

Here are the photos that I sent him as well, simple as a click on the computer and it is instantly shared. If there are quotation marks it is what was written on the back of the photo.

1st photo..."Grandma Chidseys House - Stony Creek Conn."

2nd photo...This is the photo of my grandmother and I'm not quite sure who the men are. The caption on the photo says, "3 Elm House." I saw this place when I visited, could the negative been turned around? (I have since come to understand that this is the Brainerd House. It is a great possibility that the two grey bearded men are Ebenezer and Elbert Coe.)

3rd photo... "The pier by Uncle Timmy's place a portion of his house over to the left of picture. We didn't go down there for there seemed to be people there and it is very well kept."

4th photo... "Mother this is the place you used to live and is
very nicely kept. Mother Bates was born here."

5th photo...This is the photo of my great-great grandmother and a small child in front of what is known as the Lundquist house.

(I included a 6th photo of a baptism in the local waters that I thought was interesting for R.J. but it's not relevant to this story except that it was my great grandmother's nephew, Henry Owen. The photo was very fuzzy so I have left it out.)

Seventh photo... "Harriet Coe Chidsey" (Hattie)

8th photo...Ida Mae Chidsey (Bates) my great grandmother and Ruth Chidsey Bates (Lewis) my grandmother, taken 1912 when they were said to be living in Stony Creek.

I had also included a 9th photo of Harriet's sister Ellen, (Nay, Nellie), but for the sake of the story I am leaving that particular photo out as well. I believe they were very close and there is another photo of the two of them that is more appropriate to the story. Here is one more photo that I sent the following day. It is the Summer Trolley in Stony Creek and I am sure Harriet Coe is the woman on the far right of the trolley. It is dated 1910

** Hope to hear from you soon.....I know it's a lot to take in. I haven't photos of many men and so I think the second photo may have a Coe or Chidsey man in it but I don't know.

Regards,
Bonnie **

So now I wait to see what will be revealed, and he has already responded to me that he is looking into my ancestors that lived at Stony Creek. I am thrilled at the prospects.

Aggravation

Whenever we would go to my grandparents house for dinner, we would always be expected to play games with grandfather. He loved to play Aggravation, which is a game played with marbles on a board. Whatever board we played on was always one that my grandfather had made. He would make Aggravation boards for just about everybody he knew except his family. I never did understand why we didn't have an Aggravation board at our house. He used plywood, for the most part, for the bottom of the board and he would go to the local hardware store for the top. That top would be made of a decorative formica and I think that he would often ask people what color they would prefer. He was always showing us the latest board he'd made for this person or that person. He was very proud of those boards. I remember that his was pale yellow with grey and brown paperclip looking lines scattered about on it. I have it today at my cabin. It had been poorly stored over the years before my father gave it to me, and is a little warped. That could make playing a board game with marbles challenging, at best. I am hoping that the warp eases out, but I realize, that probably will never be the case. I cherish it because it brings me memories of his intensity when playing games, not that he was always nice, but he was always intense. Having the board also reminds me of the smell that lingered in the kitchen due to the wood burning stove. The kitchen was where we usually played, and although wood stoves are not used much in California, once you've smelled that smell, that the stove gives off, you never forget it. Grandfather did not like losing when playing Aggravation, well truth be told, he did not like losing, period. It seemed like every time we played, he would change up the rules a bit, with regard to using the center spot to cut across the board. It was seriously aggravating to play the game with Grandfather. He would needle you about his win for hours, if not days, or weeks later. Grandma would never play if Grandfather was playing. She really preferred a game called Rook, and in her travel diary, she mentions several games of Rook that were played and how much she enjoyed winning. I can see how having two people in the house who loved to win so much, could become a conflict. I suppose that their common ground, that would not prove to be so competitive, was when they did their endless jigsaw puzzles together. It was always rather comforting to see the puzzle as it progressed.

In the process of going through my grandma's notes, I came to realize that photos 8 and 9 were missing. I checked through the numbered photos several times and I couldn't really remember seeing any other photo that I thought was missing. I was sure though, that I had somehow misplaced it and I looked everywhere that I could think of to sort this mystery out. (I find misplacement of things that are important, far more aggravating than losing a game, if I have played well.) I looked once again in Grandma's travel diaries and decided that the missing photos were either before she arrived in Stony Creek or after she was once there. Because of the timeframe, I knew these might be important photos to have. After endless hours of searching and turning up nothing, I went to my parent's house. I took back the first box of photos that I had borrowed and exchanged it for two boxes that I had never seen before. I went through every page in every photo book, every document, every will, every card, and in the process of doing this I found photo number 9. The joy that I felt when I saw that tiny number written on the top of the photo was exhilarating and I flipped the photo over to see what the description was on the back; it read:

May 24 - 54
"The little brown building to the left of picture is the store Aunt Nay lived in after he died. The white one in the center, which has been remodeled is Aunt Nay's house and the other porch is her place also."

At Niagra Falls on way to California 1915. Aunt Nay   Grandma Chidsey.

Well, I thought, the brown building might be the store where my grandma bought the lobsters. I had wondered what Aunt Nay's married name was. With a little research, I found that it was Howd. The photo that I have of Hattie and Nay at Niagara Falls has always led me to believe they are sisters. They bear a very strong resemblance to one another.

Since I had found photo number 9, I continued on through two more books of old photos and some of the pages were missing many of their pictures. I do not know what happened to those photos. I looked through every empty page and there before me was photo number 8. I had a complete set; the way it was meant to be! I flipped over photo 8 and found this on the back:

May 24 - 54

"This is the old home place with the widened porches and you can just see where the garage door is way over to the left just beyond the bushes then a little further to the left, at the very edge of picture you can see some leaves on the branches of the cherry tree, where I made myself sick eating cherries that were not quite ripe. You can faintly see the 3 Elm house through the porch & tree." I would imagine that some of the time those things she was writing on the back of the photos was also written with her mother in mind. That cherry tree had been there for over 50 years. Could that possibly be? What I can tell you is this; if you have ever made yourself sick from eating cherries as a child, you remember it forever and the sight of that tree surely would bring back some vivid memories to everyone who was involved.

I was very excited about my find and I wanted to get a quick email off to R. J., who had been so good to help me uncover more about Stony Creek and how my family, fit into life there. I sent the email on Oct. 29, 2012 and thought I might not get a response for quite some time as Hurricane Sandy was headed their way. Much to my surprise I found this response on the 30th:

*Bonnie, very interesting of your recent finds. I have turned nada of your stuff to the museum yet, but have a written file of all of our communications. I'm sure they'll want to see them and esp. the pics you dug up. Keep at it. This stuff does get quite detailed, if not overwhelming. Coe's were also in New Hampshire and have a famous museum type house, Concord or Manchester, (Not sure. Someone told me that from church bulletin comment). Not sure whether they would be connected with your family or not. We fared the storm fairly well. Extremely high tides (up to the front of the church wall on the street, which I've never seen before) but church sits on a knoll and wasn't even affected in 1938. Major flooding both sides, including Post Office, marina, and stores. I think some of your ancestral houses were affected, at least in cellar flooding. By no means washed away tho. Many trees down and some inconveniences. Power still not on. Nothing like NYC or Jersey here. Many inconveniences abound. Thru binoculars, it looks like Thimble made out fine, but you never know until you set foot. Water was still too choppy for any boats to go inspect.

Keep on plugging. R. J. *

That was wonderful news, and so I kept going back to the computer and trying to get updates as to the full situation in Stony Creek. By Nov. 4th I had no luck in finding whether the power was even on there yet. The cell phones were not a good way to get in touch with people and I really didn't want to bother R. J. for a few days as I was sure that everyone in town had their hands full. I wanted to do something from California and found that the timing of this story had pulled me into fully being aware of the east coast's plight. After watching the towns come together after disaster strikes, I have found that they are a resilient people there.

There has been one or two other curiosities that have come about from looking through those two boxes of photos and documents. I found a small piece of golden rod paper, about four inches square, lying in-between the photo books that indicated that my grandma had traveled back to Connecticut in 1939 - 40 and in 1954. I have proof of the 1954 trip but can't find a thing regarding 1939 - 40. It is possible that my grandmother went back to Connecticut after her aunt passed away as I have found her last will and testament and she left several items to my grandmother. My father would have been about 15 at the time and can't seem to remember his mother being gone from their home. I've given him a few days to mull it over, as I am sure that I would remember if my mother had left the house for several days, if not months, when I was a teenager. My father is 88 now but has a very good memory. I just need to stimulate it occasionally. The second curious thing that I found was a photo of Alice and myself and my sisters. I didn't know this existed, but I'm so happy that it does. It's not a great photo but brings back so many wonderful, playful memories. I'm the short one in the dress and there in the background is the long barn/chicken pen that I remember so well. My oldest sister, Linda, is to my right and my other sister, Wendy, is directly behind me. This photo was taken when we first acquired Alice. You can see that we all were fond of her. The date on the back of the photo was 1961. I do miss the color that we have in photographs today.

My grandma missed the color in photographs back then also. A charming example of that was displayed on the back of a photo that she took on her way to tour The Gillette Castle. It's black and white and shows a path that is lined with trees and bushes on each side, not much to see, really, until you turn it over. Grandma describes in detail the plants that she was taking the photo of. "June 3-54 A woodland view on the way to gillette castle at East Haddam Conn. Woods are everywhere. Some of the trees found in the woods are: Oak, Spruce, Hemlock, Locust, Dogwood, White Birch, Black Birch, Wild Cherry, Red Maple, Sugar Maple, Regular Maple, Cedar, Poplar, Willow, Hickory, Elm, Beech, Ash, Sycamore, Sumac Bush, Wild Black Berry Bush, Ferns, Laurel Bush, Skunk Cabbage, Wild Flowers in yellow, lavender, and white."

Today I take a photo and am disappointed that the color may not be exactly as my eye sees it. My grandmother wrote often in her travel journals about the colors of the leaves and flowers with a hope that those colors would become true to her again as she gazed at her black and white pictures. She describes the various varieties of foliage about her, as she doesn't see those familiar trees of her childhood while living in California. It seems to me that she is soaking up all that is about her with a desire to concretely plant those lasting memories in her mind. I believe she knows that this is her last visit to this area. I think she was a woman who viewed the glass as being half full. That is a noble way to look at life as we all know people who view the glass as being half empty. I want to challenge you to always realize that the glass is forever full......even if there is but a couple of drops of liquid inside, the remainder is filled with air. The glass, quite simply, is always full.

Camp Bethel

As I looked through the photos I came to realize that my grandma had been going to a place in East Haddam, Connecticut called Camp Bethel for years. It was one of the places that she so enjoyed returning to because, not only did she get to reunite with people she had known since she was a child but, she was able to see her childhood friend Bessie. I have a photo of them as children at this camp

On the back of this photo is written: Ruth and Ralph Bates with Bessie and Roger Bruce abt. 1900. Ralph was my grandma's little brother who passed away from appendicitis when he was ten. I have always found it so sad that Vivian, her daughter, died the same way. Back

in 1935, my grandma knew exactly what was transpiring with her daughter. Both passings must have been terribly crushing to her, as well as my great grandmother and great-great grandmother. These three women endured these passings together.

I felt that I needed to get in touch with someone at Camp Bethel and so I emailed the camp and received an almost instant response. I was curious as to something my grandma had put on the back of one of the photos she had taken in 1954; it read:

Camp Bethel - May 29 - 54
"These 3 cottages are perpendicular to the riverbank. They back up to the stairs that go down to the river. If it wasn't for the tree on the left hand side of picture you could see the river. The middle one is Bessie's cottage and where I am staying. No one is in either house in the picture as yet. In fact there is only one other family on the grounds now. This cottage was the Bates cottage." The last line on photo #23, which named the cottage, was the one that caught my eye. My grandmother's maiden name was Bates. I also had a photo (#20) of Bessie and her husband Ernest from this same trip and so I included it in my correspondence to the camp. Bessie and my grandmother had been friends since they were very small children. They had corresponded and attended camp together for years

This was photo #23

This was photo #20

I was, nearly immediately, sent a color photo of the same cottage my grandma had referred to as the Bates cottage. I can't tell you how much my grandma would have loved to see this cottage in a <u>color</u> photo and looking so loved and well kept. It was amazing for me to see it with the American flag hanging out front, newly screened in porch, and painted a butter mint yellow with baby blue trim. It looks like a little show place. It is still in Bessie's family, and that too, would have delighted my grandma. Here is another bit of trivia from the staff at Camp Bethel: I. J. W. Watkins related this story to me. "In the picture of Ernie & Bessie, they're standing in front of a Red Cedar tree. I. J. told me that she planted that tree. Her grandmother Bruce stood over her & supervised. In the early '80s, the cottage owners on the west side of Fairview Park wanted the tree removed. I refused to do it & limbed it up to about 8' so they could see the River. Everybody was quite pleased afterward.

(I was told by the camp staff that that there are stones placed in the porch that have the initials A. M. Bates. I've searched to see if that is any relation to me but I haven't found the answer to that as of yet. Perhaps I'm searching in the wrong places. I will have to dig a little deeper.)

Long Journey Home

On Thursday, June 17, 1954 my grandmother woke at 2:30 am and found that she couldn't go back to sleep. It was the day that she would start her trip to the conference in West Virginia and she was nervous about missing her train. She lay in bed until 4:30 and rose so Ernest could drive her at 5:00 to the station in New Haven, Connecticut. They arrived about 6:00 and the 6:20 train did not leave until 6:30. This train goes through to Washington D.C. and there is a chill in the air that has been colder then any she has felt during her trip. The train passes through Philadelphia and Ruth views lots of manufacturing plants. Her seat mate gives her an orange to eat and she thinks this person is very nice and lovely to talk to. This lady has <u>very</u> long hair and it hangs right between her knee and ankle. She is getting off the train in New York and my grandmother is continuing on. A new conductor gets on in New York and the train continues on to Wilmington, Delaware and Baltimore, Maryland. Her final destination for the day, comes after that, arriving in D.C. about noon.

As they near Washington she notes that it is the first time (except for thunder storms) that she is a little afraid. She has a layover of eight hours here. She starts to recite The Lord's Prayer in her mind and her fear leaves her. Once at the station, she checks her bags in a locker and has dinner. She boards a sightseeing bus and off they go to view the government buildings, Arlington Cemetery, The Monument to The Unknown Soldier where they stayed for 30 minutes to watch the soldier guard the monument. She gets back on the bus and is thrilled once they reach Mt. Vernon and Washington's home where she touches the railing and realizes that George and Martha had very likely put their hands on the same rail. She describes the kitchen and the hanging copper pots. She, too, had copper pots and I remember that she kept them shiny and immaculately clean, inside and out. She thinks the view of the Potomac River is beautiful and then suddenly remembers, while writing, that she had not been alone on her adventure. Another lady on the bus had asked her if she was traveling alone, as she was, and they became partners for the excursion. After sightseeing, this woman had to catch a different train, and so grandmother went into the station to have a meal. She ordered scallops, (might as well enjoy yourself while you can, I'm sure was her thought process there).

She doesn't make mention of it, but she must have gone into the gift shop while touring Mount Vernon and found a little sterling silver pin to commemorate her journey. I was recently looking with my mother for beads one day, as she had broken a necklace and I offered to reassemble it for her, and found this little tarnished, black pin. My mother told me to take it. "It's ugly and I surely won't wear it, I don't know where it came from," she said. I told her that it would be shiny and look like it was new by the end of the day. I thought it was Mt. Vernon but it was very hard to read. Sure enough, upon cleaning, my suspicion was confirmed and there in my hand was this little pin that, I'm sure, my grandmother loved. It is fairly worn on the edges which leads me to believe that she wore it often. I am honored to have it.

The tour bus had left her with three hours to kill in the station before her train was to leave and she would get up often and go outside to view the capitol dome as it was lit for the evening. She gathered her things and found the train track and proceeded to wait. They were allowed on the train at 11:00 pm and she put her slippers on as she hadn't slept since 2:30 am. She awoke at 7:00 am to an overcast sky in the, "beautiful hills of Virginia." They proceed through West Virginia along the New River that has many rapids and occasionally some falls. She noted that, "everything is green here." There are many streams that feed this river. They stop in Montgomery, West Virginia and she thinks it is a coal mining town because of the long shoots that stretch down to the railroad track. Upon leaving there, she will arrive at her destination, Charleston, West Virginia within thirty minutes. In Charleston she hires a taxi to take her to the church and the WHFM (Women's Home & Foreign Mission Society) meeting. I am not fully understanding of the purpose of the meeting but she was sent as a representative of her Advent Christian Church and while she was there she drank up all that was sung and spoken of the Bible.

My grandmother stopped keeping track of the dates in her journal at one point but I gather that she caught a train back to Washington and spent a little time with a friend named Helen. She was washing dishes one night after dinner and saw tiny lights outside and inquired about them. Helen went outside and caught three of the lightening bugs for her in a jar. She was completely thrilled to see them up close. Helen took her out driving in Washington D.C. again at night and I'd liken it to touring to see Christmas lights. The picturesqueness of the place was delightful to her. They also went by to see the new airport terminal and she described it in detail as she'd surely never seen anything like it in her life. I wonder if she was wishing she could fly home. I don't believe that my grandma ever flew in a plane. (It is amazing to think how quickly our world has changed over fifty plus years.) The next day, Grandma awoke at 2:00 am, ate breakfast and was off to the train station. It was a foggy day and so she dozed while on the train until 6:30 when she awoke to see Marysville, Kentucky but the fog was still thick and she could only see about 200 feet from the train. Next stop was Cincinnati, Ohio and she was taken with the large size of the station.

She boarded another train and was happy that she had decided to ship her suitcases because the ramps were long. I can not imagine traveling without my suitcases, but I guess if you are homeward bound, it could be a real convenience for you. Grandma is headed to Chicago and is thinking about going to see the aquarium there but finds that the weather is very hot and so she decides to have dinner instead. She has salmon for dinner and I'm thinking that her iodine levels must surely be increasing by this time in the trip, with all the fish she is consuming. Well, she was so happy to leave Chicago as she thought that it was terribly hot there and she was looking for a little breeze. She found that breeze as they pulled through Iowa and Nebraska which had rich green farm lands.

Grandma steps away from the train in both Cheyenne and Green River, Wyoming to stretch her legs. It is a very long trip when you think about it. I think that a five hour flight across the country is long. I can't imagine days of travel to reach a destination across country. I really should board a train to get the full feel of her travels. That train ride, should I take one, would take me places that I have never seen. Her train ride through Utah is uneventful and I can tell that she is eager to get home. She has been gone a long time and has so much to share with everyone. Sunday, June 27, 1954 is the last entry in her book. She never says that she is home, but then I guess she didn't need to, as she'd arrived back safely. I was born the following year and she went to an Advent Christian Conference in Santa Cruz, California in 1955. She came home and they were moving within months of the discovery of her church, the Monterey Bay, and the cool ocean air. Once she moved to Santa Cruz, I don't think she ever looked back. She was happy to live in such a beautiful place. Surely she realized, and was content with the fact, that it was there that she would finish her life journey.

Eulogy

When I considered writing about my family, it bothered me that my parents might not like what I had to say. Since the beginning of the writing of this account, so much has changed, and in such a short period of time too. I am sure that my mother can not understand anything that she is reading, nor can she remember what she just read, so that problem has unfortunately solved itself. My father recently had a stroke and passed away after four days in the hospital. I have come to find that the grieving process is quite a solitary one and even people who have shared a similar growing up experience, interpret their own encounters quite differently. I fully felt that someone from our family needed to speak at my father's memorial service and I had something prepared. It read this way:

"I would like to thank all of you for coming today and for your showing of support for my family. I am Bonnie DiMichele, Lowell and Nancy's youngest daughter, and I was asked to speak to you today. As many of you know, my father suffered his 4th heart attack in November 2009. I rushed up to the hospital and was sure that Dad wasn't going to make it. It was amazing how he rallied back from that. Not being sure that he might survive, I wrote the following address to help prepare myself for what might be the next step. I want you to understand that I am wearing black and white today as a statement. Dad saw the world as black and white and so I wear these colors to symbolize him."

"I have known for sometime now that these days would come.

I've pondered what it is I would say in the event of my father's passing, and how would I share my feelings of the past?

I do not want to paint an unrealistic picture of the time that has transpired.

What I can say is this; my father taught me to be as tough as nails.

I think I may have learned this at a young age while playing endless tetherball games; he would <u>never</u> let me win.

I won the game only twice while playing against him.

You'd think those victories would have been sweet, but they were so short lived that I would find defeat, soon again.

I became stubborn, I think to a degree that is not truly good for anyone.

I took away a sense of wanting my own independence.

I found that family is the most important thing in life.

Sharing love with my family, time with my family, vacations with my family, those are the memories that we create and share together.

They belong to no one but ourselves.

Dad moved and moved and moved us in one of the most beautiful places on earth.

Santa Cruz is perhaps one of the most colorful places we could have been raised; colorful in both sight and culture.

I took advantage of this place and bathed myself in all the magically magnificent moments I could, outdoors.

I have memories of the beautiful blue bay, orange & purple sunsets, bright yellow daffodils, neck breaking redwood trees, water cress plucked from the stream, little toy trucks in the sand pile, and the comfort of home during a wild winter storm.

It was safe inside, but the true adventure lay, always, in the great outdoors.

I could never get enough of being outside.

I have other memories too; those I chose not to share.

I believe that we should focus on the positives that we can find, even when faced with a mountain of negatives.

We can't go back and change the past, nor can we create more time.

I would like to say that my father knew me and that I knew him.

I knew parts of him but I failed to understand all that he was.

What I do know and wish to share with my family is this:

I love them deeply and I want them to know this truth, even if I forget to say it.

I am blessed to have them in my life and cherish all the times shared and the memories we have created.

Always turn your focus to the positives and find a way to make your world work well for you.

Don't speak poorly of people; it just makes you look really bad.

When life gives you dry roast beef sandwiches, find someone who'll trade their bologna and think they've made a great deal.

Know when to make a joke and when to be silent and supportive.

Tell the people that you love, that you love them, and let them feel your love too.

My father taught me lessons that I don't think he knew he was teaching me.

I often wish he had learned them too.

I want my sisters to go away, on this day, with a certain peace, understanding, and forgiveness.

It is the only way to successfully carry on happily."

"So, I got 2 more years with my father and I decided that now was the time to try to get to know him. You see, once memories are gone, you can never retrieve them, and that was becoming all too clear to me. When my husband and I would visit Dad and Mom, we would talk of old times and his memories. He had some fascinating stories to tell. I am so honored that he wanted to talk about everything that I was curious about. I'm sure that I will have more questions in the future but his memories are gone now. It is because of our talks that I was able to write this poem to him. I think that his favorite place to live was Santa Cruz and there are many mentions of things dear to him in this poem. At the bottom of the insert, there is mention of sandstone and sunsets. Dad built a sandstone hearth in our house on High Street in Santa Cruz. He and Mom loved a good sunset so when I saw this sandstone in The Valley of Fire, I knew it had to be the background."

If

"If heaven were a vision
Then here is what you'd see
The sparkling bay beyond us
Stretching toward the sea

The hills would shout of color
And the sun would warm the sky
We always would be happy
No tears for us to cry

The apples would hang ripe,
Upon the trees outside
The creek would flow by softly
Whilst you'd view your life with pride

If heaven were a vision
Your body would be whole
The love you hold for family
You'd freely touch and hold

The struggles that befell you
Would surely, soon be gone
If heaven were a vision
You'd fill it with a song"

"I want to leave you with one more thought; I beg of each of you, when you go from this place today, to actively search for joy. Finding joy costs you nothing in life. It is in the smallest of things, like the feeling of sand between your toe's at the beach, or peering down into a flower and realizing that no two are exactly alike, like snowflakes and people. We need to grasp and inhale the joy that surrounds us. Finding joy is free, but if you don't find joy, it can cost you everything. Once again, your outpouring of care and compassion, like the nursing staff of room 200 at Sierra Nevada Memorial Hospital, will comfort us for years. Thank You."

As the memorial service progressed, it became quite clear that the pastors of the church did not believe that my father had been "saved." I must make it clear that they were happy to take much of my father's money, and were even hoping that more would be on it's way. They led the congregation to believe that he probably was not going to any place with pearly gates. I believe that the only person who knows what is in your heart, is yourself. No one has access to my thoughts and feelings unless I allow them to know what I am thinking. Not one of us, in this life, blurts out all that we are thinking throughout our lifetime. So I come to ask you this; is it better to take a persons money, or to save their soul? I believe the answer is simple, yet it is often a fine line that is crossed by religious organizations. The church was not the only religious organization taking money for the stairway to heaven and they all knew the limitations of health, mind, and substance while they were doing this. These organizations wonder why their numbers are declining; I have no doubt why this is so. It is greed, plain and simple, greed.

I refuse to just go through the motions of life. It becomes easy to just follow and point fingers at how others are not living up to their potential. There is more to me than simple idleness. I begged the congregation to go forth and seek out joy. I didn't come out and say it, but my father never told me that he loved me, that I can remember. He had ample opportunity to say it but fully chose not to. Mom used to say that, "they both loved us," as some sort of a collective group activity or something. I realized years ago that Dad lacked the feeling of joy in his life. Being unable to experience the feeling of joy seems to suck the ooey gooey deliciousness out of your very soul. I spent my time trying to understand why Dad seemed to lack a certain fondness of people. What I learned, was that we are not destined to be our parents, if we chose not to be. We can be a constant work of improvement from our former experiences and from the places that we've been. I am so tired of people telling me that it is a generational thing. I don't believe it; surely there were many people from the generation before us that were loving people. It could have been passed down through the family line, but even then, it is a way of life that they chose to embrace or chose to change. There has been an underlying theme that I wrote down upon starting the exploration of these pages and it reads like this: "Change is good but it is equally important to have things that are consistent. Some of those constant things can bring memories flooding back into our minds and fill us with a peacefulness that is indescribable." I am all about forward movement and understanding of ourselves and the world around us. Every day is a learning opportunity and experience.

During the course of writing this book, I sprained my ankle and my physician has me wearing orthotics in my shoes. Yikes; I am becoming my grandma! My shoes do not look like hers but I am attempting to be more diligent toward the care of my feet and ankles now. I have come to find that, as we grow older, there are limitations to what our bodies can do. When you look at people who look like they don't take proper care of themselves, consider the fact that they may suffer from physical or even mental limitations. We can not change other people, siblings, parents, friends. We can only care for ourselves, and we must find the desire to properly care for ourselves. It is easier said then done for some. My father failed to care for himself in many ways. When my mother was losing her ability to reason, he still wanted her to take care of him. He may have been less stressed if he had taken over the roll that she had played in their marriage, at the time, of about 65 years. He was always looking for some one to come and take care of them for free. This was an unrealistic expectation and frustrated him greatly. Had he accepted the availability of assisted living, the stress and frustration on him could have been greatly diminished. I believe that we should not expect others to do things for us that we, ourselves, would not consider doing for another. He felt that people were looking at him as a lesser person because he had a birth defect in his right hand. My grandmother had tried to terminate her pregnancy with him by jumping off a tall ice chest. The umbilical cord wrapped around his hand and wrist and his right hand had some limitations. I am not totally convinced that the act of jumping caused the cord to wrap around his hand, but the family all thought so. He could always hit the ball out of the park and fishing certainly served him no problems. It sounds crazy, I know, but it wasn't until his last year that he talked about it often to me. I came to realize that he never felt like a whole person. His mind said, unwanted, unworthy, unloved, not understood. His mind could have said, lucky guy, great family, long life, loved. It was his choice, yet he thought it was the outside world that was viewing him negatively and acting as his judge and jury. His life could have been so very different, but alas, it wasn't. It simply was what it was, laced with a lot of disappointing unhappiness. I have learned so much from him and in such a roundabout way. Never under estimate the power of positive thought.

I have come to find that people who pass through my life are a means to always be viewing, observing, and evaluating myself, not them, but myself. I can learn from them and strive to become a better individual. In the end it is all about ourselves, that is not to say that we shouldn't help others, we should, but the only person we truly have full control over is ourself. If we want to make the world a better place we must start within ourselves. I come from a long line of people who don't easily show love. I trust, at my eulogy, that cycle will have stopped and a new system of being loved and showing love has started to develop. Now that's a big goal but it surely would be a successful ending to one's life.

Hairspray

I had alluded to some little known facts from our childhood in Dad's eulogy. I realized that everyone listening wouldn't fully understand the references, but I felt these were important to include. One of these first references was regarding the realization that our family failed to take vacations together. I did find a few photos that surrounded a trip we took to Cave Junction, Oregon many years past and I remembered that we were in the car for a very long time while looking for Crater Lake. (It should have taken two to two 1/2 hours.) Once we were there, we spent no time at all. I don't remember touching the water or even getting out of the car. Surely, we must have, but I have absolutely no recollection of it. When I queried my sister, she remembered that we had taken a wrong turn and ended up on a logging road. There was much arguing going on with regards to my mother's inability to read a map. Thank goodness for navigation systems today. You can avoid all these sorts of disasters. Needless to say, it was not a good trip and never was repeated. My sister, Linda, was just happy that the car turned around at some point and went back in the direction that we had come from. She doesn't remember seeing the actual lake either.

A story is told that Mom and Dad drove to Yosemite from Santa Cruz one Saturday, to see the place. It's about a 4 1/2 hour drive, one way, and once they arrived, they spent 15 to 30 minutes in a parking lot. Mom got out of the car and Dad did not. We are not sure if they saw a waterfall but we are fairly sure that Dad didn't want to pay the entrance fee and we could only conclude that no waterfalls were seen. Mom got back into the car and they drove home. Dad was not impressed with Yosemite. This is not the way to fully appreciate a place that you've desired to see and, hopefully, experience. That was Dad's way; then he could say, "he'd been there and didn't see what all the fuss was about." We had traveled to Oregon to see Aunt Alberta, Grandpa's sister and her husband, Orie Lee. It is one of the only times that I can recall going on a true family vacation. We did travel as a family down to Southern California for weekend visits to see my Grandma Gallagher. Now that was a hair raising ride! Dad would get in the car and proceed to pass every car possible. You may think that a natural event, but back in the 50's and 60's, the roads were two lanes and passing meant that you crossed over to the other side of the road, hit the accelerator and flew past the other car. Dad was a risk taker when it came to passing. He thought that he could judge it just perfectly. It is without a doubt that many of the vehicles coming from the other direction had to brake so Dad would have the room to finish his passing. My sisters and I would slide into the back seat, I was always in the middle because I had the shortest legs and the center of the floor, the hump, was raised for the transmission and quite higher than the rest of the floor. We all would grab our pillows and try our best to fall fast asleep. It was a terrifying ride and having your eyes wide open made it all the more anxiety ridden. I didn't like sitting in the middle but I also, always thought that it just might be the safest place in the car to be.

I realized the importance of family time, once I had my own family and we took vacations each and every summer. Most of our vacations were to Feather River Park Resort in Graeagle, California. It is a place with many cabins and the same returning families every year. The kids loved the freedom to play, hike, swim, and socialize with friends and cousins. It was like going back in time before we all became so fearful for the safety of our children. I liked it too, but it was as close to camping as I would consider coming. I believe you need to be brought up camping to fully enjoy it. I could be wrong, and now that I am older, the thought of sleeping on the ground, well, it's not my idea of having fun.

Another thought I shared was my description of Santa Cruz. The sea mist in the air throws out some of the most beautiful displays of sunset colors found on earth. The daffodils were grown by farmers up on High Street and the spring would bring a field of yellow that appeared to be reaching to the bay beyond. Henry Cowell Redwoods State Park and various other places have unbelievably tall redwoods and it was that park where we would picnic on Sundays sometimes. The watercress was plucked from our stream in Scotts Valley where our apple orchard was and the toy trucks were mine and I played endlessly with them up on High St. I have fond memories of that, and I wrote this poem to help me remember.

Rain Play

Here I sit beside the hearth
I hear the rain outside
It knocks upon the window panes
So it's here I will abide

I bring my toy trucks with me
To drive on the mortar streets
I pretend a town sits neatly
On the colored stones of wheat

I wish that I were playing
In the sandpit set outside
I see my castle sinking
Into the sand to hide

The window panes are weeping
For their covered with fine dew
My finger drawing faces,
Seem to be weeping too

For all that I am searching for
Is a finer place to play
And that will only happen
On a warm and sunny day

There was another statement that I made; "it's not good to speak poorly of others." What many of the congregation would not have known, or maybe even guessed, is that our family went through a ritual of sorts every Sunday. We would start the day by running late and Mom would be spraying her hairspray on her hair in the enclosed car. We all would be choking and Dad would be upset. The hairspray usually happened once we exited the freeway and were close to our destination. In we'd hurry into church and participate in whatever obligations we had signed up to do. After church was through, we'd pile back into the car and, before clearing the driveway, the gossip would start. Did you see this or that about whomever? Did you hear what so-and-so's niece did? You get the picture. I would think about those things that we had just heard about, during the sermon. We should be loving, kind, and considerate, and I would have the hardest time trying to figure out why that didn't seem to apply to these conversations. What was it that we were taking away from our church experience? We went to church twice on Sunday, once on Wednesday, and there were often many other times we would go. We'd go to practice for the choir, or special upcoming events, and we attended every social hour imaginable. We went to church a lot! That is precisely why we had no time to vacation. We were always busy with church. We couldn't miss a church service. That amount of dedication, didn't help us grow as a close knit family.

I made reference to roast beef sandwiches, and didn't realize that my sisters did the same thing I did everyday at lunch. Mom would make roast beef almost every Sunday before church and it would be cooking in the oven for, "Sunday Dinner," when we would get back from the church service. That roast beef was <u>fully</u> cooked by the time we returned home from church and Mom made extra so she could put it in our lunches for the week to follow. Each of us had a special way of eating our lunches. Come to find out, we all ate the roast beef sandwich first, the peanut butter and jam sandwich second, the apple third, and the homemade cookie last. It's that principle of eating what you like least, first, and saving the best for last. Mom's roast beef was dry and stringy and rather hard to chew. I was asked to roast beef dinner, early on when my husband and I were first dating. I thought it odd that we would drive two hours for roast beef, but I was willing to go along. We sat down at a very long dinner table; John's mother had invited many people to dinner. I was sitting to the right of him. I'll never forget it. I took one bite of meat and nudged his arm. "I thought you said your mother was serving roast beef," I said. "This is roast beef Bonnie," he replied. "No it's not," I insisted. "What do you think it is?" he asked. "This is steak!" I declared. He's never gotten over that. He thinks it was so funny that I thought it was steak. It was tasty and juicy; I thought it was steak. It bared no resemblance to my mother's roast beef. I still, to this day, have never cooked roast beef. I'm a little afraid that I might make it like my mother did. I don't cook anything else the same way she did, but I have a fear of cooking roast beef. It's silly really.

My father would always make jokes of situations. Because of this, I think it is important to know when to make light of a situation and when to be a comforting friend. In the last days of his life. I hope he found me comforting. I wrote the poem for him while flying to Reno, Nevada for a board meeting that my husband was attending. I had my iPad and thought it might be a valuable use of my time on the flight. I didn't really think that I'd be successful at that attempt, but I only changed two words and the poem was done. I wonder if I was thinking about heaven being a vision because I was up in the clouds. I was simply trying to visualize how I thought he viewed Santa Cruz.

A Timeline of Sorts

Grandma Ruth passed away in Santa Cruz, California 6/1978 proceeding her husband in death. She was 82.

Great Grandma Ida (Ruth's mother) passed away in Santa Cruz, California 3/1961 she was 91. She had been widowed for 22 years.

Ruth's trip to Stony Creek Connecticut was in the late spring and early summer of 1954. She may have gone on this trip for herself and to share memories with her mother.

————

Great-Great Grandma Hattie passed away in Banning, California 3/1940. She was 91 and had been a widow for about 48 years. That would have been almost 1/2 of her adult life.

Ida's husband, Wm. Goodhue Bates, passed away in California 3/3/1939 at the age of 72. Wm. Goodhue's older sister Mena passed away in Connecticut just twenty days later 3/23/1939 at the age of 75. These are the only two siblings in the family.

Ruth's only daughter Vivian passed away in Banning, California 1935 at the age of 19.

————

Ruth's family moves to California around 1912 and she is married in 1914.

Ruth bears children 1915 - 1924.

3/24/1915 (birth of a son, Ralph Warren)

Harriet's favorite sister (Nellie) comes to visit in 1915, stays for a while, and passes away in California 1/1916 at the age of 69.

7/9/1916 (birth of a daughter, Vivian)

Ruth has a breakdown 1916. Ida and Harriet move nearby to assist her.

10/10/1917 (birth of a son, Stanley)

9/18/1919 (birth of a son, Donald)

8/27/1924 (birth of a son, Lowell) This one was a big surprise (five years later) and my father.

————

Harriet's mother Louisa passes away 1891 at the age of 71 in Connecticut. Harriet's husband Lembert passes away 1896 at the age, of just, 54 in Connecticut. Harriet's father Elbert passes away 1905 at the age of 84 in Connecticut.

I can see from this timeline that there would have been certain sections of time in my grandmother's life, when continuing on with one's daily routine would have seemed hard to do. My father never knew why grandma had a breakdown but the timeline indicates that she had a son and her grandmother and aunt came to California, probably to see the baby. She is pregnant again when her Aunt Nay, still in California visiting, passes away, and then she has her own daughter and becomes pregnant again. I think this would all be a bit much for any young woman. While Ruth was still in Connecticut, her great grandmother, grandmother's husband, and great grandfather pass away within about a five year timeframe from one another. The hotels that they ran were slowing down with the invention of the car. The pull of the sunny weather in California had become something they longed for. From what I've seen in the last year or two, the weather in Connecticut surely appears to be more turbulent then the weather in California. As my father grew older, he told me of an event that happened when he was about eleven. He had come home early from school because he wasn't feeling well. He found his mother slumped over and asleep at the kitchen table. He could smell gas and saw that the stove burners were not lit. He pulled her outside and went back in and turned the gas off and opened the windows. My grandma always thought he had been sent to her by the angels on that day. While going through the photo books, I found something wonderful that had been hidden away for so many years. This tells the story of Hattie, my great-great grandma. It is her obituary and it reads like this:

"DEATH SUMMONS BELOVED LADY; FUNERAL TODAY

On Friday morning, March 15, Mrs. Harriet M. Chidsey, beloved resident of Banning, passed away at the age of 91 years, four months. She was at the home of her daughter, Mrs. Ida M. Bates of East Theodore Street, where she made her home and had been ill only ten days. Present also was Mrs. Ethel Owen, another daughter who came from San Francisco to help celebrate her mother's birthday and remained for a visit.

Mrs. Chidsey was a person of such charm and gentleness that everyone, who came in contact with her, loved her. She possessed that rare quality of unselfishness to a marked degree. She loved the flowers and birds and all nature. Mrs. Chidsey was deeply religious from her early girlhood. There being no church in her own town she went 12 miles to attend a Baptist church. Later a community church was organized in her home town with which she united. Shortly thereafter Mrs. Chidsey founded and organized a Baptist church in the town of Cheshire, Conn., to which she gave largely of her means and her talent. Mrs. Chidsey has worked untiringly in the local Baptist church of which she has been a member 15 years. She was a talented children's worker and had a special appeal to little children. She helped to organize a band of Ambassadors and taught sewing classes at the Mexican mission. She was also a member of the Woman's Union and the Woman's Bible class. Mrs. Chidsey was a member of the Eastern Star at the time of her death. She was one of the founders of that organization in Cheshire, Conn., and traveled to many towns instituting new chapters. She held membership in the Grand Lodge of Eastern Star and was chaplain of the same. She also was a member of Amaranth e. The local W.C.T.U. had a loyal supporter in Mrs. Chidsey. She seldom missed a meeting and helped unstintingly in putting over the Union's program. Mrs. Chidsey, who was Miss Harriet M. Coe, was born in Middlefield, Conn., on Nov. 25, 1848. In 1868 she was married to Lembert R. Chidsey. To this union were born five children, all of whom survive their mother. They are, Mrs. Ida M. Bates of Banning, George Chidsey of Milford, Mich., Ed Chidsey of San Bernardino, Ethel M. Owen of San Francisco, and Will Chidsey of Detroit, Mich. Mr. and Mrs. Chidsey engaged in the general merchandise business in Cheshire for 15 years, and also had charge of the postoffice. Mr. Chidsey passed away in 1896 and Mrs. Chidsey carried on the business for about 10 years. She then lived at the homes of her children. After several trips to California she came to make it her permanent home in 1915. She resided in San Bernardino for seven years; then came to Banning where she has lived these 15 years. Mrs. Chidsey crossed the continent eleven times. Surviving Mrs. Chidsey besides her five children are four grandchildren: Harold Bates, Ruth Lewis, Henry Owen, and Frederick Chidsey, twelve great grandchildren, Raymond Bates, James Bates, Willard Bates, Thelma Bates (Harris), Caroline Bates, Marian Bates, David Bates, Warren Lewis, Stanley Lewis, Donald Lewis, Lowell Lewis, Duane Lewis, and four great-great grandchildren.

Funeral services will be held in the Banning Baptist church at 2:00 p.m., Monday (today), with Rev. McKericher, pastor of the church, in charge. Interment will be in the Colton cemetery."

The flowers (many lilies) that were sent to her service were amazing and I do understand that she was as loved as it was portrayed in the newspaper article. We often think that obituaries cost a lot of money these days, but this obituary gives me such great information as to who made up her family, and it reveals those things that were important to her. Harriet had a love of the great outdoors it seems too; not unlike myself. So how close is Cheshire to Stony Creek and how can I make these bits and pieces fit together to adequately tell this story? The answers are only a curser and a click away. I am so fortunate to live in this age of technology.

It seems that Stony Creek and Cheshire are a distance of 28 miles from one another and are in the same county of New Haven. Cheshire sits alongside Wallingford which is where my Grandma lived for sometime while she was a girl. Her parents had inherited a home, around 1896, with a rear house on S. Main St. that I have a picture of. While my husband and I were traveling, we stopped to see the place. I was told that they rented out the large front house and lived in the rear dwelling which was quite large enough for the family. I believe they sold that property to come west to California. The house did not look nearly as grand today, as it did in the photo, and I was a might disappointed that we had spent the time to find it. Looking back, I'm glad we found it, and the town of Wallingford, as it was one of the places my grandma stopped and stayed for awhile, on her journey back, for the memories from her past.

This is the house on Main St. in Wallingford, Connecticut. When going through some of the photos, I remember finding a photo of a general store and I think that photo might link all of this together. When you are looking through old photos and you find a random one with little or no writing on it, it becomes difficult to understand the reason for it being included in the pile of photos. With that being said, the photos were all in a book up until my grandfather passed away and then photos were randomly ripped from the book as people desired them. A much better way of going about that would be to make copies of the original photos and give everyone their own photo book. Grandpa, Ray Lewis, passed away in 1981 and it would have taken a lot of time and energy to produce such a book then. Now I am trying to make sense of this box of photos, that is in no particular order, that has come into my possession.

This photo has this information on it, "Chidsey,LembertStore&PostOffice". I believe this is the post office my great-great grandmother ran after her husband passed away. This particular photo did not have a number on it and I assumed that it was taken at a time, other than when Grandma went on her trip. I do so believe that this is a significant piece to the puzzle of our family history. With a little rereading of my grandma's travel journal, I have discovered that this photo was indeed taken during that trip. She did not number it and include it with her memories and that may have been because she was disappointed that the store/post office was now a lumberyard. I believe it stands today, yet has been remodeled and is on Railroad Ave. in Cheshire. I have sent an email to see if I can verify this. I have found another photo of a post office in Middlefield and it is evident that the two post offices are not the same. Since Harriet was born in Middlefield in 1848, I believe that she may have lived above the Middlefield post office and that her parents may have run it as the family business. I have gone back in the U.S. census records for 1860 and found that Lembert Chidsey was 18 and living in Branford in the house of Richard and Sarah Howd and working as a farm-laborer. In 1870 he was still in Branford and it has his age as 32 (this is not correct or perhaps in 1860 he wasn't 18, these records were only as good as the record takers). He is still living with Richard and Sarah Howd and is now a waterman. I have it on record that Lembert and Harriet married in 1868 so it makes no sense that he was not living with her, but it may have taken a very long time to do the census and the thought that they were completed in a given year may be a misconception on my part. The Howd family is of significance because Harriet's sister Ellen or Nellie married Joseph Howd and I believe this is how Lembert and Harriet met.

The census for 1880 shows Lembert as an oysterman and living in Branford with his wife and four children at the time. Stony Creek is in Branford and so the census places them there. On October 8, 1891 Lembert was appointed a U.S. Postmaster for West Cheshire, Connecticut. The store appears to have been up and running since 1881 and remained in Harriet's hands for 10 years after Lembert passed away in 1896 at the age of 53. There is reference to a store being run by Hattie in Stony Creek via my grandma's notes and pictures from her 1954 journey but I have yet to fully confirm that. I wonder if Stony Creek was a summertime stop for Hattie, Ida, and Ruth. It may not have been so much of a vacation place, as it may have been a place to earn extra money. Lembert had been orphaned by the age of 10 and his uncle Samuel Rose had raised him. He had been born in Guilford, Connecticut, which is right next door to Stony Creek. I can see how all these paths crossed and how they became connected.

I have also found that the census places Elbert H. (Hattie's father) as oystering in Branford in 1860 and living next door to his cousin Ebenezer who I believe he was very close with. I've come to understand that Elbert had a house on Flying Point Ave. in 1900 as did his son Timothy who was a coal and ice dealer then. Timothy married Martha Foote (they never had children) and Phoebe Coe married Walter Foote (they had one child, a daughter). None of them had large families and because none of the families were large, I found that the family name could disappear rapidly, as I was searching the family genealogy. I have found also that one of my very great grandfathers had died in the first battle of the Revolutionary War, at White Plains New York. Had he not had 13 children, the family name could have ended soon thereafter. It occurred to me that, as a female, I and my grandmothers, could only bear our husbands children to carry their name on. We, as women, could only be the end of our surname. My grandmother was given Chidsey as her middle name but that did little to continue the Bates or the Chidsey name. (The use of those names did, however, leave clues to the past.) We can only extend our husbands name and only can we do this by having a son. The key is, having a son and your son having a son and so on and so forth. The Lewis name, even though my grandmother had four boys, is now done. There will be no more little Lewis' born in our tree. In extending your spouses name, as a woman, you virtually end yours. It makes it a little harder to find your ancestors if no one has kept accurate records. I am so grateful for the record keeping that was done by the early settlers of America. It is with records like that, that I can look in the 1904 directory and find that Elbert Coe was living at Three Elms Ave. in Stony Creek, Connecticut. This is how I know that these ancestors were from this area, I just wish that I truly knew what it was they were doing and who they really were in life. Perhaps this is as close as I'll ever get to knowing who they were, but I still hope that, when I return to Stony Creek, I will find more to discover about them.

Soul Food

For anyone who thinks about tracing their roots, you will come to find that you can discover the good as well as the sordid things from your family's past. It seems that, in many cases, every generation of my ancestors have moved or changed jobs and adapted to their surroundings to make their lives work for them. We are often told that we are what we eat and that it shows on our exterior bodies. I believe this is true to some extent. I think that looking fit is easier for some, than it is for others. One might eat exactly the same food as another but have a hormonal imbalance and look much different than the other person. I take this into consideration when I meet people for the first time. What I am looking for is not their exterior presence, but what I can pick up on, from their heart, or internal spiritual self. This speaks volumes for me because, we can all fix up the exterior of anything, it's what's inside that counts. So here we are concerned about our food consumption, all the time. The media tells us to eat this and not eat that, and what I think we really should be concentrating on is, the food we fill our minds with. I like to think of it as soul food. Even what we consume in our minds, can be the same, yet absorbed or processed quite differently by each individual person. Quite simply, we interpret things differently from one another.

While researching my family history for this book I came upon some things that were not so lovely from the past. I realized that some of those events were brought on by the great depression. It took the nation by surprise, as well as some relatives that still lived back east. The family out in California seemed to fair better and much of that was due to the work that could be found around Banning. I can say, that I do not have, "the melancholy," that has been swirling, a bit like spanish moss, through the family tree. I believe this can be avoided by the way one perceives life and one's general outlook on the world about them. There is always the state of denial that many people live in too. Many people think that if you don't have a diagnosis, then you don't have a disease. That idea just seems silly to me, but there are many people who do live their lives this way. We live in a time when we can get an accurate diagnosis and do something to improve the quality of our life. I believe it is vastly important to deal with oddities within our families. We need to seek help for those people who need assistance from the medical community. In the timeframe that I was looking back to, they really didn't fully understand what might be the underlying cause of a persons behavior. I think it is very sad when mental problems go undiagnosed. It seems that certain conditions can be inherited and if we don't confront and confirm the problem, it can just continue on and on and on through other generations. It's a gift really, to make sure that we take proper care of each other within our own families.

I must impress upon you that my great-great grandmother's love of flowers and birds would have taken her to a special place, each and every day of her life. Smelling a rose, would have been her soul food, as would stopping to watch the clouds floating by in the sky. Listening to the waves lap up on the sandy bank in Stony Creek, or placing her feet in the water off the pier, would have been her soul food. Pulling the steamed clam from it's shell and consuming it, would have enlightened all of her five senses.

It is your choice to view the world with awe or with angst. What you fill your mind with, will become your soul food. I find some of the best soul food in the tide pools of the the western shore. Tide pools and a sunset viewing, while next to the Pacific Ocean, is something I want to do daily, but I do not live close enough to the ocean for this to become a reality at this time. While I am there, I take photos and videos so I can go back and remember the amazing feelings I have when I am some place that I love, like my grandma did during her trip in 1954. I am so blessed that the videos have audio attached so I can see and also hear the waves and animal life about the coast.

A few years ago, I realized that I could not teach my children all the lessons that I had learned. That was a frustrating moment for me, for I had been hoping that I could save them a lot of time and trouble in their lives by sharing my experiences. As much as I would have liked to give them my knowledge, they were not ready to accept my learned experiences. The exercise of learning to do things correctly, or learning to correct your errors, seems essential to the growing process. I have also come to realize that people who think that they can't do things, often stop trying. I do not understand why this is, but for me, it seems that they have lost the ability to consume the good, sweet, soul food that surrounds them at every turn on this earth.

In my father's eulogy, I expressed my concern that those people in attendance would go from that place and seek joy. I had watched my father, fail to find joy in his life. I don't know if he had the melancholy, that the old family written notes had alluded to some family members suffering from. For my father, it surely was never discussed with a doctor nor diagnosed. I can tell you that the life that surrounded him, was all about him, but it seemed that he couldn't reach out and fully grasp it. I believe that you must seek to find all the beauty that surrounds you. To be a happy and content human, you must constantly search to fill your mind with the very best, "soul food," not unlike a gourmet meal. I realize too that gourmet soul food for one might be quite different for another. My husband might find his soul food in watching a ball game. I might find mine in a song. That does not mean that we can not share each others experiences or passions. Our likes are different and I might only like to share a ball game if it is played outdoors. I can then look about at nature while he consumes the beauty of the game. It becomes a win-win situation. I enjoy the one thing while he is enjoying the other. Let's face it, marriage or relationships, are give and take. It's how you manage them that counts.

If you are a person who feels that life is against you, you might not have a clue as to where to start to look for, "gourmet soul food." My suggestion is to start with very small goals. Consider them to be tiny steps in learning how to feel better. You could pick one of the five senses, (sight, hearing, taste, smell, touch,) and work toward finding a different experience or sensation of that sense each day of the week. Let's say you pick the sense of smell; each day you would go out and try something new. Sunday, you might smell a flower or many flowers to discover which scents you find most appealing. Monday, you might go out and smell different fruits at your local grocer or, even better, farmer's market. Tuesday, you might go out and smell plant or tree leaves, etc. Let your imagination get the better of you, try smelling things you've never thought of smelling before. The following week you would pick a different sense and progress in the same manner. What is most interesting is, that you will find that you will want to revisit those things you found pleasurable. Those things that you liked and that were pleasing to you. Those things, that will bring you joy. It's relatively easy to ascertain those things that are most to your liking. In discovering those things, you will be finding joy.

I said in the eulogy that, "not finding joy, can cost you everything." It can cost you meaningful relationships, knowing the true feeling of love, friendships, and it can ruin just about every aspect of your life. Remember that, "finding joy is free." You just have to actively go out and search for it. It might be a bit like putting a puzzle together at first. Those of us who love puzzles, were not always good at putting them together. It took practice and patience, as does everything that is meaningful in life.

Coda

I have felt for some time that I need to get back to Stony Creek and discover the places and the people that I have come in contact with. It's the only way to have my questions answered. The people of Connecticut have been very helpful, but I think that they would be even more interested if they were to meet me and understand what it is that I am looking for. So, what is it that prompted me to look for anything? Grandma's travel diary and photos, that's what prompted my inquisitiveness. It was that and the realization that memories can be stored in many ways but can never be retrieved if <u>only</u> stored in one's mind upon memory loss or death. I am also wondering if I will become my grandma. We are so basically different yet so much alike and some of the same things are happening to me, that happened to her. My husband and I are going back to Stony Creek this fall and I can hardly wait until that time. We will be returning during a different time of year. He can participate in a little, "leaf peeping." I have been on the east coast during fall before and found it to be a simple, complex, and beautiful place. It all depends upon the place you find yourself to be, at any given time. The countryside is simple while the cities are complex and the fall colors are beautiful and a sight that all should see at some point in their lives.

I wrote a song that sort of summed up my feelings about Stony Creek while I was writing this book. I will share it with you now as, in it's original state, it has a coda and is something unexpected for a conclusion to a book. I am not, what I would consider, an artist of canvas and paint, but I do attempt to create a picture in your mind with the use of words and notes. I did not call the piece Stony Creek, but Snowy Creek, as I wrote it in winter. I've never walked the streets of Stony Creek in winter but I've seen lots of images of the place. I think this piece possesses a certain mystery about it, as does Stony Creek for me. It is a piano piece and I hope it does embody how I look at this sleepy little town that was so active in the summers when my grandmothers walked there. These women were truly the pioneers of the women's movement and blazed a trail, although often quietly, so their grand daughters and great grand daughters would have a sense of self that was full, vibrant, and appealing to all those who would view them for generations to come. I am so very honored to be of their genetic pool. That is my sweet, from the bittersweet childhood that I had. They gave me the courage to move forward, while wearing a smile. I think I will be filled with joy, hence I walk down by the shore, at Stony Creek.

Snowy Creek

Bonnie L DiMichele

MemoryMill 2012

Postscript

In the fall of 2013, my husband and I, true to form, set off on our adventure to discover the tiny town of Stony Creek that we had left behind a few years earlier. I booked the Master Suite at Linden Point House. It was not a hotel that my grandmothers had been involved with, but it sits out on a lovely piece of property that is almost entirely surrounded by the Long Island Sound. I thought that my vantage point of the islands, the sound, and it's scenery would be excellent from that second story window. I imagined the sunsets and the views that my grandmother had seen in 1954 and as a child. I was hoping to enjoy the beauty of the area. I found so much more.

We took a walking tour of the town and discovered two of the houses that had been Aunt Nay's. The third, which was the store where my grandma had purchased the lobsters, is now someone's modern style home. I am always enchanted with older homes that display their, well maintained, age on the exterior but have lovely touches of the present tucked away inside. I was thrilled to see the houses still standing and took photos that would closely match the black and white photographs that my grandmother had taken so many years prior. We saw a beautiful sunset, found the quarry, visited the museum, shopped in the antique store, and dined in Branford. We had a splendid time, and though part of me wants to continue discovering things about Stony Creek, I've now discovered why my grandma returned to her childhood village. I wrote a poem to sum up my experience. You see, Ruth ventured to Stony Creek to imprint images on her mind. She had memories, but I think she wanted to make sure that her memories were accurate and would stay with her forever. I wanted the images to remain with me as well. That is why I write poetry; it refreshes my visual images every time I read it.

Imprints

I'm awoken in the early morn'
Light streaming 'round the shade
I wander up to see what's there
Hence the brightness that's been made

I sit upon the window seat
Staring mesmerized toward the sound
I listen very carefully
To the silence that surrounds

The moon is full and shining
Water sparkling from its beams
I wish to make a picture
For my mind to keep, it seems

Two silhouetted pine trunks
Stand imprinted in my view
Have seen a storm or two before
But to me, they are quite new

I've come to view this splendid place
As once my grandma did
I know she was returning
Renewing memories, as a kid

The granite stone beneath me
Was once used, to grind the grain
Of Indians who lived here
And the Settlers, when they came

I wonder what a child might think
While peering 'cross this inlet
The magic they would surely feel
In the image that they met

This place where I am sitting
Comes to fill me with delight
I know some day it will vanish
Erased from memory and from sight

So here, so still, within my mind
I've come to find the truth
To meet those faded images
Lovingly carried 'round by Ruth

The place where we stayed has been sold and it appears that it will run for another year for it's patrons to enjoy. I believe it is slated to be torn down and replaced by something new. I would like to return, in early summer before this happens, to reflect on two things. The morning that we left Stony Creek, we spoke with the proprietor about a lily pond that my grandmother was fond of. She sent us in search of where she thought it would be. We found it, but there were no water lilies on the pond, only hundreds of aging lily pads. It was a sight to behold, as the pond was surrounded by the loveliest of fall foliage that also reflected the yellows, reds, bronzes, and greens in it's still waters. I would love to see the pond in full water lily bloom, so to speak. I would also like to take more time to wander about the area. We found that many of the properties on the sound are now private residences. This makes it very difficult to be next to the shore. I would like to spend more time sitting next to the quiet lapping waters of the sound.

Back in 1954 my grandma had mentioned that she didn't see, "any public boats, like there used to be." The boats had been an important part of travel to and from Stony Creek when my grandmother had lived there. She noticed the change many years ago and that privatization has only grown since then. While my husband and I were searching for the ever illusive lighthouses of Connecticut, we found that many places in the state are private. It troubled me that access to the shore was kept from so many people. The silence and true beauty of the sound seems to be getting harder to view and listen to, for the general public. If much of the shoreline is private, only a very select few, ever get to fully experience it.

My husband and I also visited New York City during our travels and purposefully took a ferry out to The Statue of Liberty which stands proudly on a base of Stony Creek pink granite. I thought about my Irish grandparents and my husbands Italian grandparents immigrating to America and setting foot on the open shores of Ellis Island. That must have been a beautiful sight for them, and the act of stepping on the shore, must have felt like the beginning of fulfillment, to their dreams coming true. I was so happy to see so many different kinds of people having the same experience as I was on Ellis Island that day. It is an amazing place, and I can only suppose the depth of excitement that filled the air everyday on that island.

But with that thought in mind, I must remind myself that all things have a cycle. Perhaps the people who own the lovely privatized properties will one day leave them for all to enjoy again. Many of our forefathers left lakes, forests, parks, and other properties for all to enjoy, making sure they would be preserved in their natural manner and beauty. If that were to happen, it would be part of the cyclical pattern, that all things seem to take in life.

As cycles come and go, I am reminded that the postscript, or PS that we used to put at the end of our letter writing, has all but gone out of vogue. I wondered where it had gone to, and then I realized that it has just been simply replaced by our emoticons that we use on our tablets and phones to let someone know that they are special to us. I use them all the time, but then, I always used a PS when I really liked someone that I was writing a letter to. Everything in life has cycles, even our memories. It is my attempt to keep these memories alive a little longer by placing them on paper and in photographs. This latest journey has helped me to understand my grandmother a little better. It has also brought me to a place that I greatly appreciate and never would have known, if not for the old box of photos and the travel journal Ruth took the time to create.

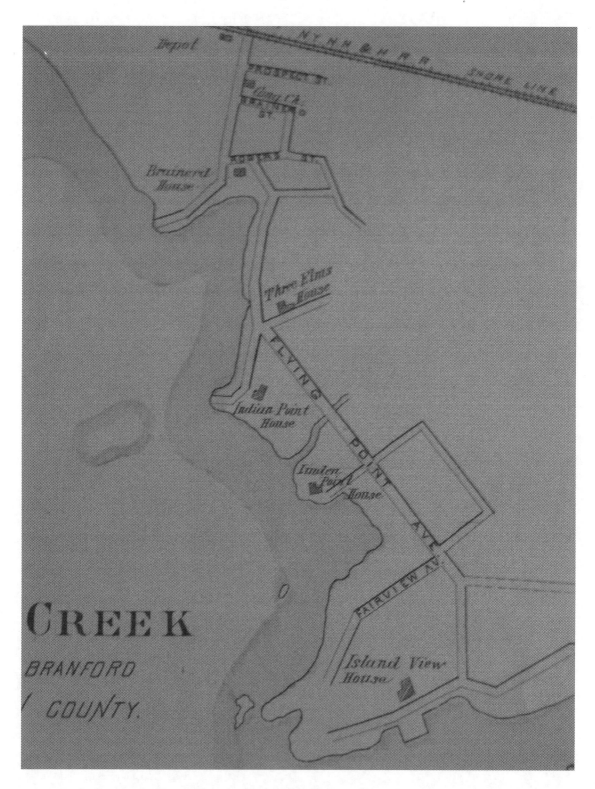

Depot

N.Y.N.H.&H.R.R. SHORE LINE

PROSPECT ST

CLARK ST

BRANFORD ST

Brainerd House

Three Elms The House

FLYING POINT AV

Indian Point House

Linden Point House

PARVIEW AV

CREEK

BRANFORD

COUNTY.

Island View House

Brainerd House, Three Elms House, and Indian Point House have had many different owners over time. The Coe's seemed to have had something to do with the running of these houses. The Brainerd House is now a private residence. Three Elms House has been rebuilt, more than once, and is now an apartment house. It is the place where I sat on it's porch and chatted with a resident during my first visit to Stony Creek. I had no idea it was one of the places that my grandmother had gone in search of, in 1954, as I was looking for the house number, (3). Indian Point House was destroyed by fire and never rebuilt. The long dock still remains and is very visible from the Thimble Island Cruise. It was once known as the Rand Point Coe's Dock.

I know that I have always lived my life with the idea that I would treat others the way that I would want to be treated. My great-great grandmother was a member of Amaranth which is also tied to The Eastern Star and their belief is in, "The Golden Rule." I can't remember my parents passing these thoughts on to me and I can only conclude that Grandma did, as it had been passed down to her from her grandmother. She must have said something to me when I was quite young about The Golden Rule because it surely has stuck with me throughout my life. Little bits and pieces can be passed on through the generations. What a wonderful ideology to live your life by, and to pass on to the wee ones that cross your path. My grandma has been gone for many years now, but I somehow feel that a piece of her walks with me everyday. The next sentiment may seem like a mere thought to some, but it can not show the depth of my appreciation; quite simply, "Thank you Grandma."